Commander C. E. V. Craufurd, R.N. (Retired)

Frontispiece]

Treasure of Ophir

"When I was a small child. . . [m]y imagination was fired by the age-old mystery of that Lost City of Ophir which furnished gold to the temple of Suleiman, and, as the years passed, I formed an ambition to discover it. . ."

In this fascinating book, the author reveals the unfolding story of his life-long quest to find Ophir. First joining the Royal Navy and then embarking toward China, the author begins a series of adventures that propel him toward his goal:

"I had fifteen more years of search, and seven further years of arranging proofs, before I was able to assert that Ophir is no longer a lost city. . . I have learnt that Ophir and the Gold of Ophir represent far more tan a lost city and a tale of romance. The lost lands of Ophir may awaken the whole of the Middle East; they may bring prosperity to a poverty-stricken peninsular that is larger than India."

Treasure of Ophir

by
C. E. V. Craufurd

Routledge
Taylor & Francis Group

LONDON AND NEW YORK

First published 2005 by
Kegal Paul International

2 Park Square, Milton Park, Abingdon, Oxon OX14 4RN
711 Third Avenue, New York, NY 10017, USA

Routledge is an imprint of the Taylor & Francis Group, an informa business

First issued in paperback 2016

Copyright © 2005 Taylor & Francis

All rights reserved. No part of this book may be reprinted or reproduced or utilised in any form or by any electronic, mechanical, or other means, now known or hereafter invented, including photocopying and recording, or in any information storage or retrieval system, without permission in writing from the publishers.

Notice:
Product or corporate names may be trademarks or registered trademarks, and are used only for identification and explanation without intent to infringe.

British Library Cataloguing in Publication Data
A catalogue record for this book is available from the British Library

ISBN 13: 978-0-7103-1012-5 (hbk)
ISBN 13: 978-1-138-99385-3 (pbk)

Publisher's Note
The publisher has gone to great lengths to ensure the quality of this reprint but points out that some imperfections in the original copies may be apparent. The publisher has made every effort to contact original copyright holders and would welcome correspondence from those they have been unable to trace.

CONTENTS

PART ONE

CHAPTER		PAGE
I.	AMBITION	17
II.	AH FONG'S HINT	32
III.	THE PERSIAN GULF	42
IV.	ARAB COASTS	59
V.	GETTING IN TOUCH	68
VI.	ON THE RIGHT TRACK	83
VII.	WAITING	102
VIII.	THE LAND OF SHEBA	116
IX.	THE LAND OF SHEBA—*continued*	131

PART TWO

I.	THE TRUTH OF GENESIS	145
II.	IN THE BEGINNING	152
III.	THE FALL OF MAN	161
IV.	THE RED RACE	169
V.	THE FATE OF A NATION	177
VI.	THE FLOOD	183
VII.	THE LAND OF OPHIR	197
VIII.	SULIEMAN	206
IX.	SULIEMAN—*continued*	220
X.	THE QUEEN OF SHEBA	228
XI.	THE LAND OF SHEBA	248
XII.	MARRIAGE OF BILKIS	266
XIII.	THE CRUISE OF HIRAM	273

PART ONE

LIST OF ILLUSTRATIONS

Commander C. E. V. Craufurd, R.N. (Retired)	*Frontispiece*
	Facing page
The Author's First Command, "H.M.S. Minto" (in foreground)	20
Dhow-building at Makalla	35
Bussorah—A port in the Persian Gulf	49
An Arab Runner	56
The Sultan's Garden, Lahej	76
Makalla	91
The Temple of Ophir	102
The Tanks, Aden	118
An Arab with his Pipe	132
Members of the Caravan	132
The Southern Gate, Sanaa	140
On the Banks of the Euphrates	146
The Wall and South Gate, Sanaa	166
A Welcome at Seihut	166
Crossing the Tigris in a Gopher	187
At Behair	204
The Temple Gate, Ophir	204
A Son of Joktan	216
Carven Stones near Sanaa	230
Sanaa from the House-top	240
The Entrance to Ibb	261
The Mosque, Ibb	261
A Ship of Hiram	273
A Ship of Tharshish	273

MAPS

The Basin Valley	181
Lands of Ophir	200
Tharshish Cruise	283

TREASURE OF OPHIR

CHAPTER I

AMBITION

When I was a small child my favourite fairy tale held no Prince Charming or Sleeping Beauty, but I loved to read and read again the charming story of the mysterious Queen of Sheba and her kingly lover, Suleiman the Wise. My imagination was fired by the age-old mystery of that Lost City of Ophir which furnished gold to the Temple of Suleiman, and, as the years passed, I formed an ambition to discover it.

A child holds many ambitions—holds them awhile and drops them, for he is easily turned from his purpose by the obstacles of hard facts. But, nevertheless, most children hug to themselves some especially treasured and secret ambition, an ideal which they fear to expose to those dread grown-ups who may take it from them and break it in pieces, or, worse still, may laugh!

Often we underrate a child's intelligence. What he chooses to learn he learns thoroughly, though how he does it often passes our comprehension. In my own case I kept my secret well, and, for fear of the ridicule that might follow, told no one. When I was a lad I would now and then take out the Old Book—but very secretively, for I dreaded the accusation of being "pi".

I was an idle youngster, always at the bottom of my class; my school reports were invariably poor, and I was reckoned stupid beyond the average. My father assured me that my one objective in life was to become an Admiral, and with sound common sense he suggested that I should first aim to become a Commander. He fondly hoped that I might even have the good fortune to command one of H.M. ships in time of war.

We had a retired Admiral living next door, and my private opinion was that admirals were silly old fools, but a Commander seemed to be a very different person, and the idea of possibly directing a warship in action was an ambition well worth striving for. Besides that, it offered a practical path for me to follow for my own private ambition. I should travel the world over and I should find Ophir.

For me there was no "perhaps" about that Ophir problem. There never has been a perhaps, though in twenty or more years of search there may have been a few passing doubts. The ambition was there and so was the determination to accomplish it.

My father taught me to handle a boat almost as soon as I could walk, and one of my earliest memories is of a small family party in a little cutter-rigged yacht. We were running free with the wind slightly on the port

TREASURE OF OPHIR

dreams of an inexperienced boy, and no difficulties presented themselves to the most junior officer in His Majesty's Navy.

Save one. Let us have the truth at any price! There was a difficulty, and a very serious one it seemed. I was not sure that I could pronounce "fore-top-gallant-sail" in a truly nautical manner. Under my arms were tucked a multitude of papers. *Ally Sloper, Comic Cuts,* and *Chums* promised full entertainment. The *Boy's Own Paper* and the *Strand* could be reserved for more serious reading. Meanwhile, that confounded "fore-top-gallant-sail" brought clouds to a sky that was otherwise serenely blue.

"Boy! Boy! I want a morning paper!"

A short-sighted and agitated old lady was peering at me through a pair of lorgnettes. In all the pride of my uniform I stood smartly to attention, whilst my hand wavered uncertainly between a naval salute and a civilian urge to raise my cap. The result was deplorable. I dropped all the papers, except one I was holding in my left hand, which I politely offered to madame. But she wanted *The Times,* and I was offering her *Comic Cuts.* Luckily at that moment my father came to the rescue as the train steamed in to end an inglorious episode.

In due course the thickest-headed cadet in His Majesty King Edward's Royal Navy was appointed to the Channel Fleet, and later, through the offices of our friend the retired admiral, to a ship newly commissioned

AMBITION

quarter when disaster overtook us, in an inlet which I think is called Bosham Creek. My father was stooping over a rope which he was coiling down, and I was peering anxiously at the peak which was swaying too freely, for my mother, who was steering, was not gifted with that skill which is the mark of the perfect yachtswoman. Suddenly the boom jibed with a whole-hearted swing and caught my father bending. Overboard he went!

If I saw such an accident nowadays I should be convulsed with laughter and crippled in action, but I rushed to the tiller and put the helm down. It was, of course, the right thing to do, for it checked the way of the boat. Incidentally, we ran slap on to a mudbank, so I cannot suppose the situation was so critical as it then seemed. Still, I had my practical seamanship tested at an early age, and that youthful training was to help me through many a year.

I obtained a success in a competitive examination that I feel was more due to the genius of the head master of my naval crammer school than to my personal efforts, and at last the great day came when a very small boy, under-sized for his age, stood on the station platform waiting for the train to take him to Dartmouth, where H.M.S. *Britannia*, the naval training ship, lay moored.

In all the glory of blue cloth and bright brass buttons I stood slightly apart from the family, who had come to see me off. My head was full of the childish

The Author's First Command, "H.M.S. Minto" (in Foreground) [Facing page 20

AMBITION

for China. Thus an ambition, already ten years old, commenced its progress towards fulfilment.

Some experts have advanced theories that Ophir is in China. Those theories are based on the assumption that King Hiram's fleet, sailing from the Middle East, must have voyaged as far as China, in order to complete their three-year cruise to Ophir. In the tropical and semi-tropical latitudes of the China coast the fleet could have obtained most of the goods which are specified for the fleet cargo.

That is about all the backing there is to the theory of a Chinese Ophir, but it was sufficient to give me an added interest in our cruise to China, though, as a matter of fact, on our way there we came nearer to the real Ophir than at any other time during my next fifteen years of search.

Our captain had received orders to "show the flag" on our voyage eastwards, and to call at Muscat. Russian activities had been rather prominent in the Persian Gulf, and the Russian cruiser *Askold,* with her three funnels, had made a great impression on the native mind. Our ship, however, possessed *four* funnels, and was therefore likely to make a greater impression. The fact that she was of larger tonnage, and had a slightly larger armament, was all to the good, but to the native mind the outstanding feature of superiority was the possession of those four imposing funnels.

One day as we were steaming in a flat calm of the

TREASURE OF OPHIR

Indian Ocean, off the Oman coast of Southern Arabia, we sighted a dhow. The day had been uneventful, and the sun was very hot as we steamed up that deserted-looking coast line. So, when we overhauled the dhow, our captain decided to break the monotony. He said that he suspected she was either a gun-runner or a slave-trading vessel. In the light of later experience I do not suppose he suspected anything of the kind. However, we closed the dhow, and ordered her to "lay to". The shrill pipe of the boatswain's call awakened all idle hands.

"Away-y sea-boat's crew."

I had the good fortune to be the fore-bridge midshipman of the afternoon watch, and therefore it was my duty to take charge of the sea-boat. "Old Charlie", as we affectionately named the skipper, called me up and gave me my orders. The good fellow made them seem very thrilling and romantic to an inexperienced young officer.

"Mind you go the weather side. If you go the lee side of a dhow the crew may cut the halliards, and let the mainsail down with a run to smother your boat. Then you will all be scuppered without a chance of resistance."

Of course the captain knew quite well that the dhow would offer no resistance, for all our starboard broadside of six-inch guns was trained upon her. Still, my eyes were nearly popping out of my head with excitement and interest.

"One more thing," Charlie called out. "One

AMBITION

more thing, my lad. Keep your eyes skinned. The *nacoda* (captain) might not be above sticking a knife into your back."

Dear "Old Charlie", what a breath of romance you gave to that hot afternoon! You had a crew of some seven hundred men, all listless and grumpy, but with your good-humoured craftiness, you made every one aboard lively and interested in what was really only a very simple afternoon exercise.

As a matter of fact, by the merest chance, we were lucky—with a beginner's luck—for the dhow was a slave-runner! Her papers showed she was bound for Muscat, but she was carrying a very large number of men, far more than her normal crew. Of course the extra men were not chained to the thwarts, nor was the *nacoda* melodramatically waving a huge stock whip. A slave-owner in real life handles his slaves as carefully as he would handle cattle, for he wishes to deliver them in good condition.

There were no papers aboard the dhow to show that she was carrying passengers, and, furthermore, passengers do not choose the month of June for travelling to one of the hottest ports of the world. Since that day I have examined several hundred dhows, but I have never again met with such a clear case of slave-running. The interpreter who had accompanied us in the sea-boat was an experienced man, and whispered to me that, as this seemed a clear case, we had better return to the ship and report.

TREASURE OF OPHIR

"Old Charlie" listened to my report with an amusement which he must have found it hard to conceal, though he accepted it with becoming gravity, and then turned to the interpreter. But if an inexperienced midshipman had rendered a report that seemed highly coloured with romance, the interpreter in emphatic but broken English brought forward such evidence that "Charlie" must, indeed, have felt that he had caught a Tartar.

Here he was, a naval captain, bound on a political mission to the Sultan of Muscat, and it seemed that he was fated to arrive at Muscat to say:

"Your Highness, I have come on a friendly and political mission. To prove my diplomatic ability, I have captured a dhow full of your slaves, knowing with what official horror you regard slave-dealing activities." Not a very propitious introduction!

After we had towed the dhow inshore we anchored and focussed our searchlights on her for the night, but by what was possibly a happy accident the electric current failed for an hour, just after the moon had dipped. When at sunrise we visited the dhow we found only the proper crew aboard. The *nacoda* assured us that the "passengers" had all gone ashore of their own free will. Under these circumstances we were left with no evidence at all, so we steamed away disappointed. Perhaps "Charlie" was not inconsolable, for his diplomatic relations with the Sultan were saved from a severe strain.

·   ·   ·   ·   ·

AMBITION

Later experience suggests to me that we had anchored that night very close to the ancient Ophir. Had I known where to look and what to look for, the silhouette of the morning sunrise would have shown me Mount Sephar, and might even have disclosed to me the citadel of the City of Ophir. As it was, my interests were entirely engrossed in the slave dhow, and so we steamed unwittingly away.

I had fifteen more years of search, and seven further years of arranging proofs, before I was able to assert that Ophir is no longer a lost city; and twenty-two years is but a tiny fraction of the time that Ophir has lain dreaming in the desert sands. Meanwhile, I have had time to appreciate some of its problems. I have learnt that Ophir and the Gold of Ophir represent far more than a lost city and a tale of romance. The lost lands of Ophir may awaken the whole of the Middle East; they may bring prosperity to a poverty-stricken peninsular that is larger than India.

We steamed away from Ophir, and that was well, for at that stage I had not sufficient experience to make good use of any knowledge that might come my way. We need experience and much misfortune before we can gain the treasures of knowledge. Ophir and its problems have given me treasures greater than I can find in any book of poetry, and the Fates were very fair to me, for, while they took me away from Ophir, they led me to the only land where I could gain clear knowledge for the full solution of the Ophir problems.

TREASURE OF OPHIR

We steamed up the desolate and rock-bound coasts of Oman and then round that prominent cape, Ras el Hadd. As we turned westward it seemed that we were steaming toward the Land of Desolation, but later I was to learn that we had actually entered the gateway of the Cradle of Civilization.

You will remember that Genesis* states there were four rivers which came to a junction near the Garden of Eden. The Euphrates was one of those rivers, and the other three seem lost to geography. The Euphrates flows into the Persian Gulf, and the nearby lands hold many legends of the lost Garden. I was not out to discover the lost rivers, but one of them was an important clue to my problem—the lost river Pison, which "compasseth the whole land of Havilah", for Havilah was a tribe mentioned in the same verse of Genesis that gives the first allusion to Ophir. During my first visit to the Persian Gulf I gained very little information, but I did, however, gain one useful hint, and that under circumstances which seemed singularly unpropitious.

We had left Portsmouth in April, with the band playing "The girl I left behind me", while the sun shone bright between the April showers. It was June when we steamed into the picturesque and rock-bound harbour of Muscat, a brazen sun shone overhead, and to an unseasoned crew it seemed to be the hottest place in the world. The sick-bay was full, and many officers

---

* Genesis ii, 10-15.

AMBITION

were down with fever. I was very fortunate, for I seldom get sick during hot weather, so perhaps I may give a few hints to those who, like ourselves, were facing excessive heat for the first time.

While the sun is down it is good to drink copiously, though, of course, one must use common sense and discretion in the use of alcohol. While the sun is up it is well to drink little and to eat but little. Mahomedt the Prophet, on whose name be peace, knew his lands, and left many sound instructions to his disciples. He himself ate so little that he often tied sun-warmed stones to his waist to stay the pangs of hunger.

He bade his followers fast from the first ray of dawn until sunset during the whole month of Ramazan, which comes in the middle of the hot season. I have never attempted to keep the full rigours of that fast, but out of consideration for my servants who do, and would find it trying to prepare food during their hungry hours, I am careful to confine my day meals to a light breakfast, with, perhaps, a cup of tea and a biscuit during the day. The result is very beneficial to one's health.

In those earlier days, when first I met the Persian Gulf heat, I did not know these things, and failed to realize that you can do the hardest of work with very little food during an Arabian summer day. Certainly the conditions were very trying. During one forenoon our Chinese steward, who had been ashore for provisions, opened the serving-hatch to the gunroom, and called us to "come and look-see". It appeared that the eggs were not quite so fresh as the bazaar Arab had suggested, and, as a matter of fact, one of them was in process of hatching out! We were, however, delighted, for that chicken would have made a ship's pet of which we should all have been proud. Unluckily, none of us had the first idea of how to rear chickens. We thought the poor little chap must be hungry after chipping his way out of the shell, so we tried to feed him on white of egg, with the aid of a pen-filler, but he did not long survive our kindly experiments, and, with a feeble cheep, turned up his toes.

That afternoon we had a more grim example of the power of the Arabian sun. A dhow had been working from seaward into the harbour, but during the afternoon the wind failed, and she lay some three miles distant, very picturesque, with her lateen sail drooping in graceful folds. Toward sunset the evening breeze helped her, and she crawled slowly into Muscat harbour, where the remnant of the crew told their tale of a tragedy of which we had been the unwitting participants.

They had run short of water, and were overjoyed when they saw a British ship lying at the outer roadsteads of Muscat harbour. When the wind failed they tried to signal us, for they knew that directly we learned that they were in need we should send them all they required. Alas! by the time they got as close to us as the failing breeze would permit, they were too far gone to summon sufficient energy to make any vigorous signal

AMBITION

and so attract our attention. All of the crew, except two, perished of thirst while help lay close at hand.

We had our own tragedy that evening. Among the sick seamen was one youngster who had contracted pneumonia through sleeping in the launch which was stowed on our boom deck. There is no danger in sleeping out in the open during tropical weather whilst at sea, but you must keep the stomach covered, for the night dews of the Persian Gulf are very heavy. This youth had neglected the advice given to him by the older hands, and though in a normal climate he might only have contracted a chill, yet in the Persian Gulf, with his system run down, his chill rapidly developed into a critical case of double pneumonia. We carried him to the chart-house on the after-bridge. It was the coolest place in the ship, and the officers were sleeping on this after-bridge, while we kept the chart-house for the sick man.

On that hot night we slept but lightly, and an hour before the dawn there was a stir in the chart-house. We knew the doctors were fighting against odds, and the chaplain was at hand. As the first rays of dawn came slanting through the rock-clefts of Oman on the Arabian shore there was a weak coughing, then stillness. The doctors had lost their battle.

I sat up and smoked a cigarette. The grim rocks grew bolder in the growing light, though the rays of dawn still softened their hardness, and made of them things of beauty.

TREASURE OF OPHIR

"I will work to develop this land," I vowed.

Looking back, it seems to me curious that I should have formed such a resolution at such a time, yet it was a good one to hold to, and without that resolution I should not have learned from Arabia the secrets she held, nor have discovered the key to the riddle of Ophir.

Muscat held no consecrated ground for Christian burial, and we therefore decided to give our friend a sea burial. We looked through the dead man's effects to see what to send home, for it is the custom at sea to collect the private property of the deceased, and sell by public action anything that is not likely to have sentimental value. Some article of clothing is held up by the auctioneer, and bidding proceeds rapidly. Quite frequently, when it is knocked down, it is thrown back again to be re-auctioned. By this means all the ship's company have the opportunity to contribute funds to the relatives of the deceased, while property with non-sentimental value is conveniently disposed of.

Searching through his property we made a rather curious discovery. It was a letter written by a girl friend of his. She begged him to be very careful, as she had dreamed that she saw him sleeping in an open boat, and that he had died, and been thrown overboard to the sharks. It was a curiously accurate warning of what actually occurred.

That night we steamed eastward, out towards Ras el Hadd, and with solemn naval ceremony committed his body to the deep. Looking back on that incident

AMBITION

now I can trace a curious link between the death and burial of that young seaman and the furtherance of my quest.

His dying cough had awakened me before the dawn, and with the swiftly following sun came my ambition to work in Arabia. At his eerie funeral, amidst summer lightning and distant thunder, his last dive to the depths started a train of thought which I followed up, and which has been of material assistance in solving a very difficult point in the reconstruction of the past and in proving my discovery of Ophir.

You may look at an Admiralty chart and follow what that incident suggested to me. East of Ras Mussandam there is very deep water. Pass through the Straits of Ormuz and into the Persian Gulf, and you will find that the depths of the Persian Gulf are not those of an ocean.

It took me years to develop that hint and all it implied, and it was the only important evidence with respect to the Ophir problem which I gained during my first visit to the Persian Gulf.

CHAPTER II

AH FONG'S HINT

WE were very pleased when a telegram from the Admiralty ended our work in the heat-laden Persian Gulf, and ordered us to proceed eastward on our three-year commission. Of course, at the age of eighteen, I did not take my Ophir problem, nor any other problem, too seriously. I was very happy to see all that the world had to show me.

Looking back, I am amused to find that the quest seems such a romantic one, for when puzzling out details day by day, and year by year, that aspect was not so prominent. That is the way with the Book of Life. Romance is always on the next page until we reach middle age. After that the shy goddess seems to have retreated to the earlier chapters. We rarely note her figuring and posing on the page on which we are working.

When I started on my quest I soon realized that I had many advantages and some handicaps, though at that time I could not see the handicaps very clearly, and so imagined that the difficulties which I could foresee were the only ones I should have to face. On the other

AH FONG'S HINT

hand I could see some of the tremendous advantages that were given to me. Other investigators had to travel the world at their own expense, and in their spare time, but a naval officer may travel over most of the world, and the only expense he will incur is a possible loss in professional advancement. Such considerations did not trouble me at the time I was a midshipman of eighteen, in a ship of war eastward bound.

I was certainly in the one profession in which I could gain the full qualifications for finding a lost seaport, for in a sense that problem frequently faces every navigator, for when he has been at sea some days he cannot be absolutely sure what the winds and currents have done to his ship. If cloudy weather or fog intervenes he is to some extent lost. He knows the position of his destination, but he cannot tell its exact direction, unless he knows the exact locality of his point of departure at the time he is setting his course on the open sea. He must apply the various arts of navigation to fit his case.

"Old Charlie" was the best of naval captains for training under. He required every midshipman in the ship to give him a noon-day position when at sea, and he took a great deal of personal interest in seeing that we used our best endeavours to learn every intricacy of navigation.

If a midshipman had been unable to take the morning observation through lack of opportunity or sheer laziness, he had to "cook" his sight in order

TREASURE OF OPHIR

to show up a well-seasoned dish. Knowing his rough position, he would work backwards, assuming an astronomical time, and by mathematical calculation he could find a fictitious altitude that would produce an astronomically fixed position to suit all assumptions. Applying this to the Ophir problem, I was qualifying myself to find Ophir so soon as I could find a reliable point of departure, or, conversely, I was becoming qualified to fix a point of departure and a good deal of intervening information, if the Fates put me at Ophir and then left me to prove that I had got there.

Whilst we midshipmen were learning our work, the ship, under more responsible navigators, was making her way to Colombo, a port which has frequently been suggested as the original Ophir, the main claim to that suggestion lying in the fact that it is a good market for ivory, apes and peacocks.

There are, however, several difficulties in making the available evidence fit the facts, the main difficulty being that of fitting the cruise of Suleiman's fleet from Palestine to Colombo and back again into three years.

It is suggested that Tharshish, which is mentioned in connection with Hiram's cruise, was the Tarsus of New Testament history, and the point of departure of the fleet. Assuming that in the days of Suleiman there was no connection between the Mediterranean and the Red Sea, the fleet would then have had three years to sail from the Mediterranean round Africa to Colombo and return to Tharshish in the

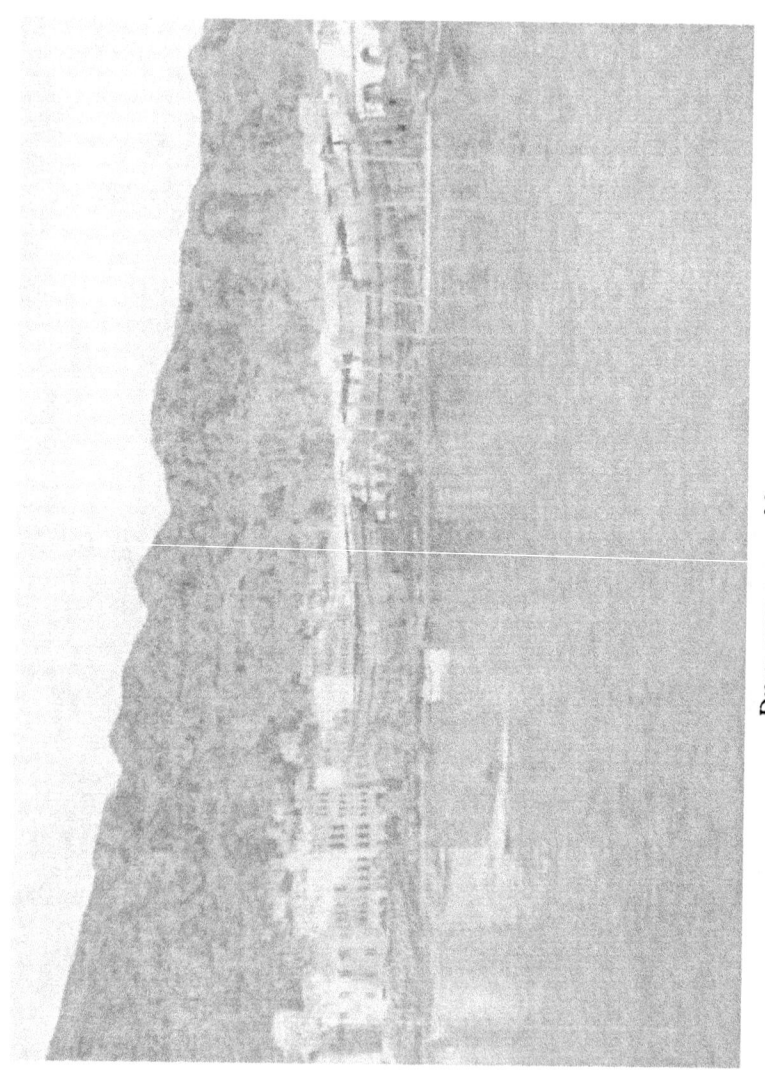

Dhow-building at Makalla

[Facing page 35

AH FONG'S HINT

Mediterranean. That suggestion seems fairly feasible, though the cruising time is overlong, if taken direct between the two ports. Unfortunately there is no satisfactory evidence that Tarsus was actually the point of departure, and, further, there is a strong suggestion that there *was* connection between the Mediterranean and the Red Sea in the days of Suleiman.

There is another very strong point against this theory. If Colombo was originally Ophir, where was the Gold of Ophir? There are many other minor objections, but if we enumerated them all we should be in the position of the polite Spanish officer, who wished to apologize because his out-station fort was not able to return a salute that had been offered to his flag. " I have so many excuses to make," he explained. " To begin with, we have no ammunition." With one overwhelming explanation, why trouble about small details?

The opportunity to examine the Colombo-Ophir theory from personal observation made the port doubly interesting to me. I had spent all my pocket-money, and was in my normal state of being "stony broke", but that did not matter, for it was not on shore that I was likely to gain any valuable information. What I needed was some information about the native ships. Did they give any evidence of earlier designs? Was there anything to suggest the ships of Tharshish or the ships of Hiram? Were they fit to round the Cape of Good Hope, or to undertake a three-year voyage? I

TREASURE OF OPHIR

had not formed my questions so definitely, perhaps, but I did realize the importance of knowing something about the ships of Suleiman, so as to gain the utmost information from the description of the three-year Ophir cruise.

There were no deep-sea vessels in the harbour; the south-west monsoon swell was breaking heavily against the harbour breakwater, and throwing up great mountains of surf. We watched the little outrigger canoes dashing out to sea with one man at the helm, and the other perched on the outrigger, using half a coconut to dash water up to the peak of his little calico sail, so as to make it hold the breeze to the fullest. We gave to them the whole-hearted admiration of one seaman to another who is handling his boat to perfection.

Outside Colombo we met a fishing fleet, and saw that the native type of vessel is a light craft, rather fast, but not sufficiently sturdy for prolonged cruising. Certainly I had not found the cruising craft that interested me from the point of view of my quest. As a matter of fact, one month earlier I had seen off the Arabian coast the very craft that should have told me all I needed to know, had I but realized it.

We steamed onward to China, and there I hoped to find some further interesting evidence, for though Ophir has been mooted as being up the Persian Gulf, notably at Kishm Island and Karachi, Colombo and Calcutta have also been suggested, and, as already said, some investigators have suggested that Ophir

AH FONG'S HINT

may possibly be somewhere in China. Each of these theories has raised the question: "Where is the Gold of Ophir?" China is a very large country, and it is known that there is much gold there, but it is very far from the Kingdom of Sabbaea, and it seems difficult to connect the Queen of Sheba with far Cathay.

We arrived at Hong-Kong somewhere about August. Hong-Kong, with its teeming life, quaint buildings, gorgeous shops, and the beautiful Chinese ivory carvings, was sufficient to fill a midshipman's interests. Ophir and its riddles had a rest for a while, and then came forward with redoubled force.

In those days a midshipman's main duty was boat-sailing, so we had every opportunity of perfecting ourselves in this art, for our boats were of different rig, and included the cutter rig that Captain Bligh had made so famous when he sailed across the South Seas after the mutiny of the *Bounty*. I took great pleasure in this duty, and it awakened again my desire to learn more of ancient ships and their capacity for long voyages, but it looked as if I had come to a full stop in my investigations.

The only chance that I could see of learning more about ancient ships was to find some book that dealt with old-time navigation, or to examine those excellent models which are exhibited at the Royal United Service Institution Museum. I was well acquainted with that museum, for when passing out of H.M.S. *Britannia*, a

TREASURE OF OPHIR

naval pensioner at the museum had helped me to learn the knots, splices, bends and hitches that are amongst the first items of a seaman's education. Alas! the Royal United Service Institution was three years' distant at the end of the commission in China. But the unexpected happened, and old Ah Fong came to my rescue.

Ah Fong was a kindly pig-tailed old gentleman, a Chinese merchant who owned the most attractive shop in Queen's Street, Hong-Kong. He well knew that a midshipman's purse is drained long before the end of the month, but that made no difference to him, and he always welcomed me to his shop, for I think he liked showing his treasures to an appreciative pupil.

On one occasion he taught me the use of the Chinese counting-machine, and many times that knowledge was of service. I used to go to a Chinese or Japanese shop and bargain fiercely. When the owner felt the bargain was approaching cost price, he would produce his counting-machine, make the beads fly up and down while he calculated the wholesale cost price, the retail expenses, and then, with a flick or two, add the minimum profit he would accept. Secure in his knowledge, he would be prepared to close the bargain so soon as my offer exceeded his calculated sale price. With the help of Ah Fong's information I could note the minimum price, and then offer one or two cents in excess.

With my chum I strolled past Ah Fong's shop, conscious that the one dollar twenty cents in my pocket was to see me through the month, and could buy no

AH FONG'S HINT

treasure from his window. Ah Fong was standing at the doorway, and welcomed us in.

" You likee see ship pickshur?" he queried, producing some quaint oil paintings.

My chum and I admired the pictures, and I asked how it is that a clumsy old Chinese junk, with its coconut-matting sails, can outpoint almost any European sailing vessel. We thought the Chinese had borrowed their designs from the old Portuguese navigators; but Ah Fong smiled, and, opening out in his quaint pidgin English, explained that it was far otherwise. He quoted dates from Chinese histories, and pointed out that the Cantonese junk is modern in comparison with the northern Chinese junk, though, even so, the Cantonese design is far earlier than anything known in the European history of navigation. He took us to the back of the shop, and showed us two beautiful ivory models of the Northern and the Cantonese junks. Their difference in rig was obvious, but he showed us the difference in lines, and explained why that difference existed.

Again referring to Chinese histories, he told us that the Northern junk is of a design many thousand years old. We laughed at his statements, for his dates placed the design well before the great Flood. However, Ah Fong was quite sure of his information, and he told us that the Chinese were not the original designers, but had learned their arts from some country of the Middle East. In less than half an hour Ah Fong had taught us far

TREASURE OF OPHIR

more about the designs of ancient ships than I have been able to learn from many years' study of Western literature.

"You wanchee buy pickshur?" Ah Fong queried.

I turned to my companion, but he was no wealthier than myself.

"I shall have to wait till next month, Ah Fong," I sighed. "I have only got one dollar, twenty cents."

"All 'i. Can do," answered Ah Fong, and pressed three pictures into my eager hands, paying no attention to my astonished protests.

Two of those pictures are hanging in front of me as I write, and remind me of all that Ah Fong taught me that happy afternoon. He explained how sailing-ships of the present day hold many of the essentials of those earliest designs, and how to trace from these onward to the ships of Hiram and Suleiman, and thence to the present day.

.   .   .   .   .

The China commission drew to a close, and at the end of three years we returned home. For the next few years I drew blank. I searched many of those semi-religious, romantic works which try to base history on myth, hoping that they might give some hints on Ophir, for it is evident that the City of Ophir was founded many years before the reign of Suleiman. They seemed to give no information of any value, but a long course of that study helped me to devise some method of working,

AH FONG'S HINT

and to gain some instruction even from works that seemed to deal with entirely mythical matter. Furthermore, that type of literature helped me to the habit of reading closely, and so to extracting detail from what often seems very meagre information.

Meanwhile the Zimbabwe ruins had attracted a great deal of attention, and information on them was published in detail. The theory that Ophir was situated in East Africa seemed obviously incorrect, for Ophir lands were somewhere near to Havilah, and Havilah was encompassed by the lost River Pison. No stretch of imagination could take the river Pison down to East Africa if it had a junction with the River Euphrates. I absolutely discarded the Zimbabwe theories of Ophir, and in that I was wrong, as Professor Keane, with his splendid book, "The Gold of Ophir", was to prove to us.

Among other suggestions, Ophir has been placed in South America. I had the opportunity of visiting Buenos Aires and Rio de Janiero, but got no glimpse of Ophir, nor any hints to help me in its discovery, though I certainly had a very enjoyable time there.

CHAPTER III

THE PERSIAN GULF

In due course I received the offer of an appointment to a ship in the Persian Gulf. Of all the officers and men who were appointed I suppose I was by far the most keen, for once again I could gather up my threads of evidence and examine them off the shores of the land which was most likely to hold Ophir secrets.

One of our first duties was to police the Bahrein pearl banks, and while studying pearl-fishing methods I gathered most valuable clues.

Pearl fishing takes place during the height of the summer, and it was a typical Bahrein morning when the cry of *"Salaam Aleikoom"* rang out from our forebridge. The interpreter, with a huge megaphone to his mouth, was hailing the pearl fleet which we were approaching.

" *Salaam. Salaam Aleikoom,*" he hailed in sing-song voice, making his greeting ring far over the glassy waters. The fleet was at anchor and the dhows were crowded fairly close together, for the pearl bank they had selected was a small one.

" *Salaam. Salaam Aleikoom* " (Peace. Peace be

unto you), he called, the usual greeting of the Persian Gulf.

The crew of the nearest dhow collected together, and a few seconds later the cry came booming back from forty deep-voiced Arabs:

"*Aleikoom Salaam.*"

Until the peaceful greeting has received reply it is not etiquette to proceed with conversation. Indeed, I have known such lack of courtesy to be answered with a rifle-shot instead of with "*Aleikoom Salaam*" (Unto you be peace).

It was dawn and the divers had not yet commenced work. They were digesting the breakfast which they take before sunrise, and they were washing it down with many a cup of Kishr, that delicious drink made from the husk of the coffee-bean. They would not taste another meal and would swallow no further liquid until sunset, when the day's work was finished. This abstemiousness has nothing to do with the religious fasting of Ramazan, but is necessary because the pearl-diving is very hard work, and any food or drink during working hours causes vomiting.

We were steaming to the fleet to ask if there was any small service we could do for them. We tended their sick and frequently supplied them with drinking water, for pearl dhows usually stay on their banks until their drinking water is exhausted. Consequently the appearance of the British patrol-ship is very welcome, for the dhow crew work on a profit-sharing basis and are very pleased to gain a replenishment of water supply that will permit them to stay longer on the pearl bank.

We asked if there were any sick, and one of the dhows replied in the affirmative. We stopped the ship preparatory to lowering a boat, but the sick man saved us all trouble by simply diving overboard and swimming to us. The doctor asked what ailed him, and he replied that he had a cold disease and required warming: for among the Northern Arabs there is a general classification of hot and cold diseases. This man probably had a chill from too much diving, but in his own mind his disease required no careful diagnosis. He was sick, and his profession made him immune to any hot disease, for he was diving all day, actually spending far more time under water than above; therefore he knew that he had a cold disease.

Amongst his own people he would have been burnt with red-hot irons, and, though the cure sounds primitive, it is usually a very effective one. The women undertake most of the doctoring, and, incidentally, I have found they have a good general idea of blood circulation. The patient was very shy, but we persuaded him to come to the sick-bay. Unluckily on the way there we passed the blacksmith, who was busy beating out a red-hot iron plate for repairing the funnel of the steam pinnace. The sick man gazed in horror; certainly he had a cold disease and required a hot remedy, but this was above the odds. A dive, a splash, and in two hurried strokes he reached his own dhow, safe from

THE PERSIAN GULF

those fierce foreigners and their crude methods of doctoring.

We steamed on, the interpreter busy with his hail of "*Salaam Aleikoom*". Then he informed us that the admiral of the pearl fleet was a friend of his and offered us hospitality. We accepted with pleasure, and if I had realized what was in store my own enthusiasm would have been more marked. As we rowed to the pearl fleet flagship the dhow crew grouped up. We clambered up the ship-side, to find friendly hands stretched out to help us to the deck, and as we stepped aboard there was a low-voiced welcome of "*Koom*", an abbreviation of "*Salaam Aleikoom*". Our host led us aft to some cushioned seats on the poop, while one of the crew came with an earthen flask of piping-hot Kishr.

Of course, we immediately asked about the pearl-fishing, and Ahmed Salem, our host, explained the methods, which are very simple. The diver wears horn pincers on his nose, to prevent the ingress of water, and on his fingers and toes he puts leather shields. The object of these rough gloves is to prevent his fingers and toes from being cut by the sharp oyster-shells while he is groping on the bottom. Around his waist he wears a small basket, into which he shovels the oyster-shells. He stands on a stone, to which is tied the lowering line, and in his left hand holds a communication cord, which he tugs if he gets into difficulties.

"Now watch the diver breathing," cautioned Ahmed.

TREASURE OF OPHIR

The extraordinary thing about an experienced Bahrein diver is that with practice he seems not only to inflate his lungs but also swallows air right down into the stomach. He is generally a man with an enormous chest-development but with little chest elasticity.

"How long do you think a diver can stay under water?" asked Salem.

We suggested anything up to one and a half minutes, for we had all heard of the wonderful diving abilities of a Bahrein Arab.

"Well," said Ahmed, "this water is very deep for diving. This bank is thirteen fathoms. Measure it for yourself, so that you shall be fully satisfied. In more shallow water I should expect a diver to be able to stay under at least three minutes."

We had brought with us a lead-line to take soundings, and also a couple of stop-watches, so as to time with absolute accuracy. The diver inflated himself with many deep breaths, and then held up his right hand.

"Splash" went the stone and "click" went our stop-watches.

There was a pause while the second-hand circled round. The interval grew long and then very trying. What had happened? The depth was seventy eight feet and the second-hand had completed the circle. Surely a man could not remain all that time under water at that great depth? But still the second-hand circled round.

THE PERSIAN GULF

We looked from one to the other, and we looked at Ahmed, fearful to break the silence when he might need to issue some quick order, for a man's life hung in the balance. When the hand of the stop-watch came to one minute thirty seconds the silence seemed almost unendurable. We well knew that there are sharks and swordfish in those waters, though a diving fatality is of rare occurrence.

One minute forty. One minute forty-five . . . fifty. Surely the worst had happened?

Then the Arab tending the line began to haul in quickly. His practised eye had caught sight of a body floating upward. The diver broke surface and the two stop-watches clicked almost simultaneously. One showed one minute fifty-five seconds, the other showed one minute fifty-five and two-fifths seconds. We helped the diver aboard; he was somewhat exhausted, but in a very few seconds was his normal self. He showed us his basket, which was well filled with oysters, and proved that he had been at the full depth all the time.

We were also shown how the diver gropes his way on the bottom, feeling both with hands and toes for the oysters, hardly trusting to his sight in those dark depths. All the men readily answered the doctor's many inquiries, and the most interesting answer came when he asked about the effect of deep-diving on the ears. It seems that the diver needs to burst an outer drum before he can dive to any great depth, for the pressure on the ears is very painful until that outer drum is burst. However, it has no marked effect upon the hearing.

Ahmed explained to us the basis on which the pearl-diving is carried out. No diving-suits are allowed on the banks, for there would then be a danger of their being cleaned out, whereas at present they are merely gleaned and recover during the off-seasons.

We asked why the Bahrein pearls have such beautiful colours, for they are generally superior to those of other banks; and Bahrein pearls are the most valuable, though not the greatest annual yield, in the world Ahmed hesitated before giving us the answer, for he was afraid we would laugh at his information, which has been gained by many generations of pearl-divers.

"It is the fresh water on the banks," he explained. "You know that in Bahrein Harbour there is a great fresh-water spring which wells up from the sea-bed?"

We had heard this was so, and later we often watched the natives obtaining their water in the most original manner. While the dhow is at anchor in the harbour, the diver slips overboard with an empty goat-skin bag and dives a couple of fathoms below the surface into the fresh-water spring. Then he opens the mouth of the bag, which, of course, he closes before he reaches the surface.

"Yes," continued Ahmed, "there are fresh-water springs in many places of the ocean-bed. Of course, we can only detect some of them. Fresh water has a

BUSSORAH—A PORT IN THE PERSIAN GULF

[Facing page 49

THE PERSIAN GULF

great effect on the colour and brightness of the pearls. It acts as a sort of tonic to them."

That explanation seemed to us to be somewhat far-fetched, but I certainly have found that the Arabs know a lot more about pearls than we do. That information about the subterranean fresh water of the Bahrein Banks gave me an important clue as to the lost rivers of Eden, and I may mention here that Arab information generally helps in unravelling ancient history which has been regarded as myth.

. . . . .

The climate of the Persian Gulf is somewhat trying, but life at that date was full of incident. There was a certain amount of gun-running and slave-trading, and if the patrol of the Banks was not very constant there was apt to be a murder or two. The season before we had the patrolling of the Banks there had been a rather lurid murder, and this eventually led to some fighting, in which we took part.

An Arab informer had been giving the British authorities some information about gun-running, when, unfortunately for him, the news leaked out that he was giving information against his friends. He tried to cover his tracks by hiring a pearl dhow and shifting every evening from one pearl fleet to another, but his enemies got on his tracks; they also hired a pearl dhow, and one evening they succeeded in tracing him out.

In the middle of the night a canoe ran alongside

and requested Hassan, the informer, for some water. The request was a very usual one, for pearl dhows are continually running out of drinking-water. Hassan and his mate were bent over the drinking-tank with dipper in hand, when, with a swift stab in the back, the mate was despatched, and before anybody could awake sufficiently to offer resistance, all the dhow's crew were butchered, with the exception of Hassan. They took him prisoner and bound him to the anchor of his own dhow.

"It is the duty of the captain to watch over his ship till death," they explained, giving him full time to inflate his lungs, and then they slowly lowered the anchor, careful that he should not have his life shortened by injury against the coral bottom.

With diligent inquiry our Political Officers traced the crime to Tangastani instigation, so we sent to the sheikh of that tribe, demanding a fine as penalty. He answered with language that was more forceful than polite, and in consequence we had a little fighting with the Tangastani; quite a friendly little scrap, and we tried to conduct it in a gentlemanly manner and in accord with accepted Arab customs. After all, we were merely out to get the fine from the Tangastani, and there was no need to create bad blood about a little work-a-day incident.

We used to land at one of their fishing villages a little before sunrise and make an early start, because we did not want them to fire on our boats before we

THE PERSIAN GULF

had disembarked. The Arab starts his day punctually at sunrise, and in no case were we disturbed in our disembarkation, provided we started our work early enough. Then we would have a jolly day of target-practice, each side taking cover behind sand-dunes. We had the most ammunition, so were able to drive the Arabs back to the villages.

The obvious method of punishing the tribes seemed to be to cut down the village date-trees, but our Political Officers assured us that this is against the rules, a fact I have lately corroborated by study of the Holy Q'ran. Having driven the enemy off, we used to launch any fishing-boats we found and hold them to ransom. We always retreated at sunset, for our force was small and we had no desire to be rounded up by the tribe under cover of night.

Towards the end of our little campaign the Arabs on one occasion put up a very poor scrap. Some three days later they sent us the explanation. Their letter was to this effect:

> Sorry we did not put up a better show. We had run inconveniently short of ammunition. However, we are quite ready now, if you would care to pay us another visit.

At another village we heard they had a new dhow, which they did not want us to capture, so the sheikh summoned all the womenfolk, and they carried the

TREASURE OF OPHIR

dhow inland and back to its building-cradle. They must have spent a very hot Sunday forenoon, and we felt rather sorry for them when we went ashore, drove off the villagers, and captured it after all. We tried to launch her, but had to hurry over the job, and unfortunately broke her hopelessly.

This minor campaign gave us plenty of hard work and healthy exercise. His Majesty was pleased to grant us the Persian Gulf medal and bar, though, unfortunately for me, a pet monkey got fooling around and lost my decorations. Years later, when I was talking one day to Sheikh Awad of the Tangastani about old times, I happened to mention how I had lost my souvenir of Tangastani days. The next morning he sent me a very quaint coffee-pot from those lands, and it is, of course, one of my most treasured possessions.

With gun-runners and slave-traders we did not have much luck, for their communications were very well organized. However, we did have one rather amusing incident as we were steaming out of the Shatt el Arab and down into the Persian Gulf. We were on our way to Muscat, and were not patrolling for gun-runners, when we passed very close to a dhow, which gave us a hearty hail, to which we replied and swept on. Later we learned that she had been full of rifles and that on sighting us had assumed we were after her, had hurriedly jettisoned all her cargo, but used such small marking-spars that they sank, and she was unable to recover a single rifle. One may imagine her

THE PERSIAN GULF

chagrin when we passed her and did not even make an attempt to search.

Shortly after this date I had the good fortune to contract acute appendicitis. Of course, appendicitis is seldom regarded as good fortune, but in this case I had no reason to curse my luck. I was hurriedly run up to Basra, the Basra of Turkish times, where there was an American mission hospital. Not only have I to thank the surgeon, his wife and the hospital matron for an excellent operation and for their very kind nursing of my case, but I am able to look back on many an amusing incident during my stay under their hospitable roof.

One morning the doctor told me that a favourite rug of his had been stolen. I felt very sorry for him, for he kept so few possessions and really gave his all to the Arabs, so I suggested he should send his boy down with a note to the Turkish Governor. The Governor took the matter in hand at once, sent for the hospital staff, and soundly flogged two Arab men-servants. The poor missionary was very distressed, but I admit that I did not share his feelings, for the rug appeared back in his study within a couple of hours of the punishment.

At that time I could not talk one word of Arabic, so after my operation I lay in bed, very exhausted and unable to speak to any of the Arabs who lay near. Later the doctor managed to get me a ward to myself, so I lay quiet till sunrise. One day a large number of

TREASURE OF OPHIR

Arab women collected outside my room with a sick man whom they had brought in for treatment. They kept pointing to me, and I heard the word "*hakim*" (doctor) frequently repeated. They had decided I was the doctor, and they objected to seeing me lying quietly in bed while they had a case requiring urgent attention. They stormed into the room, intent on turning me out, but fortunately for me the Indian nursing sister came up just in time to save me from an awkward predicament.

There were many interesting incidents at the hospital, both humorous and pathetic, and I will mention two of them before picking up the main thread of my story.

The matron, who had but recently come out from her home lands, one day appealed to me because Hamoud, one of her staff, was giving trouble and seldom turned up to his work punctually. She said it was no use reporting him to the doctor, for the missionary was too kindly a soul to deal severely with any man. The matron was a pretty lass, so, of course, she got her way. I agreed reluctantly to attempt, with the aid of the interpreter, to get Hamoud to mend his ways.

Amongst Hamoud's other sins, he was in the habit of marrying and then divorcing his wives as soon as he had spent their marriage dowry.

"Look here, Hamoud, you ruffian," I explained, "you must give up these little recreations if you are

THE PERSIAN GULF

employed by a Christian missionary, because it might give the firm a bad name."

Hamoud promised to mend his ways, and quite agreed that if he turned up late again he should get the sack. Next day he limped in about two hours late, and I told him he must play fair and realize that he was dismissed.

"I have not come here for work," said Hamoud. "I am sick and I want to see the Beautiful Lady."

I suggested his reputation would hardly run to an interview with the Beautiful Lady, and that he had better first tell one of his own sex what were his ailments, but Hamoud would not tell me his troubles, so the matron granted him an interview. She came back looking very amused, but said she could not tell me Hamoud's ailments without his permission.

"It is all your fault," he complained to me. "You preached about my having several wives when I was connected with a Christian establishment, so this morning when I woke up I took my three wives to the street and publicly divorced them."

After that, feeling he had done a good morning's work, he had smoked a cigarette and returned to his house for breakfast, but his recently-divorced wives had reached there first, and the breakfast he got was too hot for his liking. Zenab stood behind the door and tripped him up, and Zuleika sat on his head whilst Zahra wielded a big stick.

Now that the Beautiful Lady had repaired the

damage Hamoud suggested I should act as a friend and use my good offices with the Cadi to get him remarried to his lost wives, who were ladies of character. I did my best for him, and the Cadi explained how Hamoud could regain all three wives after he had paid the full penalty for his hasty action. Knowing Hamoud, I doubt whether the story had a conventional happy ending.

About the time my surgical wound was mending and I was able to move about a little, the doctor came in one morning with his face full of trouble. He had been working all night trying to save an Arab who had been mauled by river sharks. The river sharks of the Euphrates are quite small but so very voracious that they are extremely dangerous. Motaen had stepped out of his canoe to haul it up the mud-bank, when a shark attacked him and bit the calf of his leg. In a moment the blood had attracted other sharks, all small fish, averaging two and a half to three feet in length. They worried at his leg, and by the time his friends had come to the rescue the calf was only hanging by a few sinews. All that night the doctor had been working to join up the torn muscles, and now the leg was turning septic.

"I shall have to take his leg off," the doctor explained "if I am to save his life. Come and see if you can persuade Motaen to undergo the operation."

I went to the ward and saw Motaen lying patiently, though the gangrene had set in and the flies were buzzing. I tried to reason with him, and you may be

An Arab Runner

THE PERSIAN GULF

sure our conversation was quiet and patient, for he was in the presence of Death. I told him that if he would not consent to the operation he would be carried out a corpse within two or three hours.

"It is not that I fear the operation," he explained. "Personally, I am quite willing to submit. But my wives have explained to me that if I lose a limb like this I shall be a living disgrace, and when I die, though I may ascend to Paradise, no houri would comfort me in my eternal loneliness, for I shall be one-legged, as I left the earth."

Nothing I could say would shake his belief, and I could not help but respect the faith of a man who was prepared to sacrifice his chances in this life in order to ensure his position in the next.

"Good-bye, Motaen," I said, giving him my hand. "You are a brave man and a good Moslem. May Allah reward you," and I left him to die in peace. Could I have done otherwise?

The hospital was very full, and the British Consul very kindly invited me to stay with them so soon as I could move. I used to sit on the Consulate veranda, watching the busy river-life, and one afternoon my hostess pointed out to me a curious boat and told me it was the Euphrates gopher, the oldest type of ship known to history. It was, indeed, a quaint craft, a sort of huge circular basket pitched within and without with native bitumen. "Make thee an ark of gopher-wood," says Genesis, and the translation would perhaps

TREASURE OF OPHIR

be more accurate if we read : " Make thee an ark-gopher of wood," for it is evident from the original language that this amended translation would be permissible. I had gained yet another link in the chain of evidence to establish the identity of Ophir.

I was to obtain yet another before I left the Persian Gulf. You will remember my friend who splashed overboard to the deep waters off Ras el Hadd. His hint led me to study the depths and observe the landfall as I crossed and recrossed the Persian Gulf, and it soon became evident that the Gulf with its lowland shores was once a basin valley surrounded by high mountains. This basin valley theory is one of the most important links in our chain of evidence.

CHAPTER IV

ARAB COASTS

LIFE in the Persian Gulf grew rather monotonous. Gun-running appeared to be slacking off, we had no news of slave-traders, everybody was on good behaviour, and the heat was very trying. We had not much news from Europe and were somewhat out of touch with Reuter.

Then one hot evening the Captain called me to his cabin. A confidential telegram had come through, and as we deciphered it our interest grew, for it was the warning telegram before the declaration of the Great War.

To the regular officers of some years' seniority the news came as no surprise. Equally with the Germans we had been preparing for Der Tag for many years, and if there were any regular officers who really thought the coming war was going to be a short affair, they had not read their history aright. Even so, we who were on the out stations felt many pangs of regret for from childhood onwards we had trained with the idea always in mind that we should immediately be called to service when our country was in the hour of need.

TREASURE OF OPHIR

When that hour struck there were officers and men on out stations all over the world wondering whether they would have full opportunity to serve their country to the best of their abilities. Now that it is all happily ended I do not think that any one (however bemused or bemedalled) would wish to go through those four years again. Of my personal experiences I consider that only the humorous ones, and those that indicate Arab life and character, are worthy of record.

We hurried our little ship to Bombay at her pitiable average speed of about five knots, though by setting a topsail we gained about ten per cent. on that. She was a paddle-wheel ship and we called her the *Ocean Bicycle*. For patrol work she was very useful, but her guns were worn out, and she had no real fighting value. We hoped to get to Bombay in time to pay her off, and, without crew, to commission a more modern craft.

On reaching Bombay I was given the command of a small ship, H.M.S. *Minto*, and my duties took me up the Red Sea. How proud I was of my war command! To me she was the finest ship in the King's Navee, and, though she had some obvious defects, it rested with me to smooth over her blemishes to the best of my ability. Her total broadside was 6lbs. 1oz.; so slight, in fact, that there were critics who did not take her quite seriously.

The gallant Captain Cochrane, of Nelson days, had faced a similar difficulty, and had triumphed, so I took him as my naval hero. On one occasion he made his crew paint their faces black, and by that simple ruse surprised and defeated the enemy. Eighty per cent. of my crew were dark skinned, for they were lascars of the Royal Indian Marine; but if that ruse of Cochrane's was inapplicable, there was many another trick which I might take from his book. He had a false armament, and often he used false colours until he was within range of his enemy. Above all, he employed an unfailing sense of humour, an example the humblest of his disciples might try to follow.

My decks would not stand a heavy armament, but a few old canvas gun-covers, stuffed with bottle straw, and stiffened with broom-handles, made excellent gun-barrels, while some casks of peas served for gun-mountings. By these means we seemingly trebled our armament in one joyous forenoon.

The bluff sounds a childish one, but it had its value when dealing with bedou chiefs who had never seen a naval quick-firing gun. It seemed to lend to our little ship a true Cochrane air, and with grave sincerity we were able to assure our Arab allies that, though they could see our ship bristled with guns, we could honestly promise them the full support of a hundred ships even better armed than ourselves.

On one occasion when we were entertaining a party of Arab dignitaries, I was thrown into a state bordering on nervous prostration by a stout sheik, who would persist in wandering about and leaning heavily against things. Time and again I prayed him to be seated, for the chances were two to one that he leaned against a dummy gun, and they were not constructed to withstand heavy strains.

My Second-in-Command hovered in his vicinity, ready at any instant to dash to the opposite side of any collapsible structure to apply counter-pressure, and thus maintain the prestige and dignity of the British Navy. We heaved sighs of relief when our corpulent friend finally ruined his sash by brushing against a freshly-painted barrel of peas, which was serving as a gun-mounting, for after that he was content to be seated.

Our first war orders were from the Commander-in-Chief, and very thrilled we were as we decoded one cipher number after another. As one man we faced the stern realities of war, and checked each word with eager intentness.

"Proceed up river, and endeavour to intercept s.s *Adler*. She is cargoed with German beer, but her cargo should be fully examined."

Panting with eagerness, we proceeded on our way, fully determined to act in accord with our instructions in every detail. To our lasting regret I have to state that the gallant enemy completely outwitted us, and succeeded in gaining neutral waters.

After this mild-and-bitter failure we were sent to Aden, and lay restive and impatient in the harbour, envying those who had real war work, and wondering when our opportunities would arrive. One night a long cipher message came through, and it was about 2 a.m.

ARAB COASTS

by the time we had deciphered our orders. We were informed that Turkey had come into the War, and we were directed to collect up all Turkish shipping that we could intercept. Full of joy I sent for the Chief Engineer, a man many years my senior, and an officer well experienced in Red Sea waters.

"Come on, Chief, wind up the old bus," I cried, as I led him to my cabin, and showed him the orders.

"You know this coast well enough. Where shall we make for?"

"Make for Jiddah," he advised. "All the Turkish shipping will be thereabouts at present, for the pilgrim season is on now."

Jiddah is a harbour literally strewn with coral reefs, and as we had never visited that port, we used a simple strategy for entering the harbour under safe navigation. I sailed in under Turkish colours, keeping the British ensign bent and ready for breaking directly we undertook any warlike action. The Turkish Governor sent a pilot to conduct the supposed Turkish warship to her inner anchorage, a matter of some difficulty since he had removed all navigation marks, and thereby imprisoned such British shipping as was in the harbour waiting for our Indian pilgrims who had just returned from the Haj at Mecca.

The pilot stepped aboard, and I have never seen a man so startled as he was whilst I conducted him hurriedly to the bridge. We let his pilot launch go, for we were after bigger fish than a mere pilot.

TREASURE OF OPHIR

"Captain," he cried, "this is not a Turkish warship."

By good fortune I had in my pocket a pipe in a soft leather pipe-case.

"No, it isn't," I answered quietly, pressing the pipe-stem into the unfortunate pilot's ribs, so that he thought it was a more dangerous weapon. "No, it isn't, but please navigate very carefully, for we don't want to have any accidents."

The good fellow took us to an excellent anchorage, and for the next three days we retained his services, and he proved invaluable to us, though somewhat under compulsion. Meanwhile, the port launch had returned, and to our joy our signalman reported that the Turkish Governor was coming to call on us. As yet we had committed no warlike action, for the pilot was a civilian, and pilotage is a peaceful occupation. Now, if we could entrap the Turkish Governor, we were ready enough to resume our proper identity, so our signalman stood ready to break the White Ensign.

We stood crouched behind our guns and our barrels of peas, but the wily Governor had his suspicions, and turned away when within a hundred yards of the ship. Fortunately I had sensed that there might have been some international agreement regarding this pilgrim port and its Haj season, so I did not open fire on the Governor, but awaited events. Ten minutes later the Port Doctor came to call on us, so we then broke our

ARAB COASTS

colours, and retained both the doctor and the port motor-boat.

The doctor was very amused at his predicament, but he did not tell us anything about international agreements, of which he must have been well aware. I think that wise Governor was waiting for us to commit some warlike act which would have entitled him to retain some forty thousand Indian pilgrims, British subjects who were returning from the Haj.

We wrote a polite letter to the Turkish Governor, and stated that we were retaining the doctor and his motor-boat, as we had some sickness aboard; further, if the Governor would be so kind as to send off to us the British Consul we should be delighted to expedite the return of doctor and motor-boat. The Turkish Governor sent a very courteous reply, regretting that we were delaying the return of the doctor, since plague had broken out in the British pilgrim camp, and the only doctor available for work in that camp was at present enjoying the hospitalities of a British warship.

One up to Old Man Turk! With an effort we redoubled our politeness; we wrote thanking the Governor for his care of our pilgrims, and we suggested that, under the circumstances, British pilgrim ships must not complain if they were overcrowded; meanwhile we were sending the doctor ashore by a shore-boat, as the motor-launch had developed minor engine defects which we were repairing; still we awaited the arrival of our Consul.

TREASURE OF OPHIR

The harassed Turkish Governor greatly desired the return of his smart motor-launch, and he welcomed a British suggestion for overcrowding British ships that could not leave a port which had all its navigation marks removed, and was known as one of the most difficult harbours for navigation. He sent the pilgrims aboard the ships in harbour. The British Consul had already left Jiddah, but he sent us the sub-consul with all his papers, and we returned to him his motor-boat, freshly painted with our best enamel.

The Governor had forgotten that we were still retaining the services of his pilot, who during the next two days kindly conducted all our shipping out of the harbour, together with some forty thousand British subjects. Delighted with our week's work, we wirelessed to our Commander-in-Chief requesting further instructions.

The answer was a red-hot one, and somewhat unexpected. During the Haj season Jiddah was to be regarded as a neutral port. The presence of a British warship in Jiddah harbour was most undesirable. It was rumoured that a British warship had been flying false colours. Did we know anything about such undesirable proceedings? We were to return to Aden and report.

At Aden I found a stern-visaged Admiral, and I was so busy quoting the precedents of my naval hero, who had used false colours on occasion, that I quite forgot to mention such minor matters as a few thousand tons of British shipping and the forty thousand pilgrims.

ARAB COASTS

While making my report and explanations, I fancied I saw a smile hovering around the lips of the Admiral, and I should not be surprised if it was so, for he was in truth the kindest-hearted chief under whom I have had the honour to serve.

Immediately after the Jiddah incident we received orders to proceed to Hodeida and endeavour to bring off the British Consul. We had reason to believe that Hodeida held a heavier armament than our own, so we were careful not to arrive there till close on sunset, when the light was growing bad. We sent to the British Consul, but unfortunately he was unable to come to us, so we sent to the Turkish Governor demanding immediate evacuation of the town under threat of bombardment at daylight, and we set fire to a dhow which had some Turkish stores aboard her.

Our bluff succeeded well, and at sunrise we had the pleasure of seeing all the inhabitants evacuating the town under our terrible threat of a broadside of 6lbs. and 1oz. Unfortunately, we only had nineteen white officers and men aboard, so we did not feel that we could spare a garrison to make good our capture of Hodeida harbour. Later, when I gained the friendship of the ex-Governor of Hodeida, he told me that his garrison were awaiting events just outside Hodeida, and would certainly have recaptured the town. Further, he told me that the only stores of any importance were a gramophone and four records which had just arrived from Constantinople for him.

CHAPTER V

GETTING IN TOUCH

During my work on the Assir coast I learned a great deal about tribal life and organization, as well as of curious examples of Arab custom and mentality, information which proved very useful to me in my work, both then and later. On one occasion I had a rather striking example of the tricks that chance may play on the ignorant.

I had arranged to rendezvous with a sheikh ashore, and instead of saying that we would meet one or two hours after sunset, we compared watches, and agreed as to the time we should meet. I arrived punctually, and waited several hours without result, but next morning the sheikh reproached me bitterly, saying that he had waited at the rendezvous most of the night. Only when we compared our watches did we find what was wrong.

We Europeans count our time from an astronomical midnight, while the Arab commences his day at sunset, so that the time is roughly six hours different. To make matters more complicated, the sheikh was using the figure six as his zero point, and when I objected he remarked:

GETTING IN TOUCH

"You hold a frying-pan by the handle, why not a watch?"

One sherriff gave us a lot of unnecessary trouble, but I finally got even with him. He sent urgent word that he was in difficulties, and the Turks were pressing him so hard that he doubted whether he could hold out the night. Navigating in coral waters, when one is pressed for time, is no joke; but when we arrived, all hot and bothered, the sheikh merely sent word that we need not have troubled. He thought he had been poisoned by Turkish intrigue, but his stomach ache had got better.

I sent a chit to our doctor, which read:

"The sheikh complains that an ass has been poisoned. Would you kindly mix up a box of horse-balls?"

To the sheikh I sent my own medical directions, which were:

"Take one every two hours until confidence is restored."

We had no further trouble. Later on I told this tale to an appreciative audience of rival sheikhs.

Once when some unfriendly Arabs had been giving us a little trouble, a big sister came to our aid and fired some six-inch shells, while we fired our little pop-guns. Altogether we did not do much damage, but we were quite content if we frightened our foe. Unfortunately for the villagers they had a wise man, who told them that he would return our fire, and, under his direction,

TREASURE OF OPHIR

they salved a dud lyddite six-inch shell and carted it back to their market-place.

"You put fire behind it," he explained, tapping the shell, "then you will find it goes off with a bang."

So they built a bonfire, and awaited results. But as nothing happened, they went off to supper, and later on returned to group round the bonfire and discuss the day's events. Unfortunately they returned just as the shell had warmed up, and it proved the truth of the wise man's sayings. The survivors regarded this as a particularly dirty trick for which we were directly responsible.

One of our duties consisted in patrolling outside a Turkish seaport on the Red Sea coast. The sky was blue, and the sea was blue, and I began to feel rather that way myself after a month of it, for no adventure seemed at hand. For political reasons I was carrying some Arab guests aboard and of course was careful to extend the small hospitalities, such as the forenoon cup of coffee, which the Arab gentleman appreciates.

One morning a sheikh approached and delicately informed me that my guests wished to scold me, and hoped I would not take offence.

"We know well that you are in the habit of going ashore and interviewing Turkish garrisons under flags of truce, but you really must not do things like that," said the spokesman; and all the guests added a chorus of assent.

"You should never trust a Turk," he advised, and

GETTING IN TOUCH

added many gruesome tales, which I suspect were exaggerations of the truth.

"Thank you, sheikh," I laughed. "You are not the first person who has told me I shall get cooked and eaten for breakfast; but I don't believe it, and, anyway, if it does happen there are plenty of better eggs in the basket," and I left him to puzzle out my mixed metaphors, for a happy idea had struck me, and I wanted to work out some of the details.

Why on earth should I patrol outside that rotten little Turkish seaport? I would go and ask the Town Governor to give me possession of the town, and I thought it quite likely that if I put matters in the right way he would grant my request. His town was surrounded by my Arab allied forces—certainly several days' march from the town, and very reluctant to come any closer, but I saw no need to emphasize the fact.

I dressed myself in my Sunday best (not forgetting a clean white handkerchief), and invited my Arab guests to come ashore with me, and hold a little arguing match with the Turks. They indignantly refused, though my interpreter was delighted to accompany me in search of adventure. So, waving my white handkerchief, we pulled for the shore, where a Turkish sentry politely helped us out of the boat, and took us prisoners under our white flag. The boat's crew then paddled out of range awaiting my signal for return. Meanwhile, in answer to my wireless request, other ships were hurrying to the entertainment which I had promised to provide.

In a few moments the Turkish Town Governor welcomed me at his headquarters, which we reached after a few hundred yards of blindfold walk.

"*Effendi*," I pleaded with impassioned tones, "your town is surrounded. It is true we are at war, but I do not want you all to have your throats cut in your gallant endeavours to defend yourselves when hopelessly outnumbered."

I thereupon drew a map, showing the Beni Ahad to north, the Beni Ethnein to south, and, wholly blocking his eastern retreat, I showed the powerful Beni Thalatha. If my drawing was slightly misleading, I have never claimed skill of draughtsmanship. I talked on and on, while I watched the sun growing more yellow with the approach of evening. All worked out nicely to plan, and I knew the senior naval officer with his fleet would now be showing plain on the horizon.

"Should I come ashore to tell you such details, if I did not know that your position is hopeless?" I exclaimed, glancing at his impassive face, which told me nothing.

The sun was now low, and so I played my trump card.

"Perhaps you doubt my word, *effendi*? Then I give you my friendly proofs. You have just time to bid your scouts saddle up and get into touch with my Arab forces before sundown. But I strongly advise your men

GETTING IN TOUCH

to return before nightfall, for if our searchlights show us any men on the roads we shall certainly open fire."

I paused to light a cigarette before proceeding in a leisurely manner with the conversation, for I knew that, unless he had penetrated my bluff, he must surely show some signs of impatience.

"*Effendi,*" I smiled to him, " I know that I have the honour to talk to a very brave man, and my suggestion is an attempt to help you in your dilemma. I see, however, that you will not surrender without a fight, though your guns are so outranged that you will be able to make no reply to our bombardment, which will take place to-morrow at sunrise. Good-bye, and good luck, *effendi*. Please note that we shall use our utmost endeavours to avoid harming the mosques. Your Jumma mosque shows well from the sea. Good-bye, *effendi.*"

A few slight signs of restlessness had shown that the *effendi* was feeling uneasy, and that meant he was inclined to believe my tale. He would have time to saddle his force, ride hard, and tire out his under-fed mounts, then either attempt to fight his way through hostile country, or return to the town with his cavalry too tired to escape the next day.

Meanwhile, in high feather, I returned to my ship in time to report to the senior naval officer that the Turkish garrison would probably shelter in the Jumma mosque, and the town would surrender after a short bombardment.

TREASURE OF OPHIR

Next day, when again under a flag of truce, I collected the Turkish garrison, my friend the gallant *effendi* drew me aside. " Commander," he said, " you gave me friendly hints; now let me return the compliment. We know that you are in the habit of going amongst the Arabs. Do not trust them too far, for I could tell you many tales of their treachery." I thanked him in my broken French, and I realized how mutual misunderstanding had brought Turk and Arab to bitter enmity.

It was in a curiously unpropitious manner that I first met an Arab chieftain who afterwards became my firm friend. One day, whilst at Aden Residency Office, making my report, the Assistant Resident walked over to a small scale map, and with the point of his pencil traced an area of about five miles.

" Could you go over there?" he queried.

I looked at the place, and saw that it was well inside the Farisan Bank.

" Certainly not," I replied. " That is supposed to be the most unnavigable area in all the salt seas."

" What a pity," said the Assistant Resident, pulling at his pipe. " What a pity! We particularly wanted you to go there."

When he explained what the needs were, I realized that this was no light-hearted request, and, though in times of peace I should not have felt justified in taking the navigational risks the job offered, I had full justification for undertaking anything in war time.

GETTING IN TOUCH

Briefly, he wished me to act as postman, and deliver a letter to a small Arab seaport, where resided a very important Arab chief, whom we wished to make our ally. If we succeeded in getting through the innumerable uncharted shoals and coral reefs of the Farisan Bank we were supposed to send the note ashore by a local fishing-boat, which would bring back the answer—if the chief were sufficiently friendly to frame an answer.

Only the week before, when we had sent a boat ashore to visit a friendly sheikh, it had been heavily fired on.

"What sort of chap will this be?" I asked the political officer. "Will he be friendly, or is he likely to hand out a surprise packet like the last man?"

"I will give no guarantees at all," he answered.

The first journey to Gizan, that small seaport of the Farisan Bank, was an anxious one. By diligent inquiry we found one Somali who had once visited Gizan in a British warship, and he informed me that they had grounded on coral nine times in one day. Our ship was a frail one. A previous examination of the rigging had shown that the foretopmast was rotten at the heel, and we had no opportunity to replace it, and only that morning a lascar had knocked a hole in one of the plates when scraping old paint from the ship's side. When the First Lieutenant had reported the matter, I praised the lascar for his diligence, but gave the order to knock off scraping. Now the First Lieutenant came along with a further suggestion.

"I know, sir. We will tell them to put on all the paint they can. It may glue the old bus together a bit."

If the ship had her failings, I certainly had the finest set of officers and men that any naval officer has had the privilege to command. If ever there was a risky or disagreeable job to be done, we never insulted anyone by suggesting that volunteers were required. Each man did whatever turned up, and never made a song about it. The lascars would heave the lead, working in the chains under the full heat of the Arabian sun for two hours at a time. When we were in coral waters an officer would keep watch at the mast-head looking for coral reefs, well knowing that if he failed to spot a reef the crash of grounding would shake him off like a ripe apple, and the rotten foremast would probably follow him.

When we got to Gizan it seemed to me there would be little sense in sending a mere letter ashore to an Arab chief. Confidence or distrust are reciprocal, and if we wanted an Arab chief to help and trust us, we must show that we fully trusted him. When we arrived at Gizan a sheikh at once came off to call on us, so I gave him the letter for the chieftain, and said I would come ashore to receive the answer, so soon as the Seyidt was ready to receive me. The Seyidt Idrissi, the chieftain in question, sent reply that the day was

The Sultan's Garden, Lahej

[Facing page 76

GETTING IN TOUCH

Friday, the Moslem Sabbath, and, as the day ended at sunset, would I please come ashore after that time? I replied that I would call again later in the week.

We left the harbour and returned on the Monday morning. This time the Seyidt sent word that he had fever, but that in the cool of the evening his fever usually abated. Could I make it convenient to call after sunset? I had as yet no guarantee of his genuine friendliness, and under the circumstances matters did not look too promising.

I felt that it was important to find out what the Seyidt's attitude really was, and if it was unfriendly to bring matters to a head. So I replied that, as I was representing His Majesty's Government, I should expect a full guard of honour to receive me. I reasoned that this procedure would necessitate him showing his hand and, if there were any dirty work, the true story would soon reach our Political Service, since there would be plenty of witnesses to tell the tale.

The Seyidt sent his wazir with a courteous reply to the effect that, as matters were still in an extremely confidential state, His Highness thought that a full guard of honour would set too many tongues wagging. Clearly the Seyidt had no intention of seeing me in daylight. Either I must return to Aden with a letter which would give no convincing proofs of his sincerity, or I must meet this chieftain after dark, and find for myself, by practical experience, whether his alleged friendship was truly sincere. I decided on the latter

TREASURE OF OPHIR

course, and that night, shortly after sunset, for there is little twilight in those latitudes, I was rowed ashore.

It was a beautiful calm night. A quarter moon was showing and throwing the Gizan hills into bold relief that seemed black and forbidding to me. I had given the order to muffle the oars, and when the boat grounded, I bade the crew row out again to deep water, out of sight of the shore. The night was beautifully warm, yet I will own that the first European to land in Assir found his teeth chattering. The wazir met me, gave me silent greeting, and then conducted me to an isolated house, up some stairs, and past two blind corners.

By now I realised that if any treachery were intended my case was hopeless, and felt very glad I had not brought a revolver, which is a very uncomfortable burden, and moreover, I felt sure that if I had carried one I might easily have let it off at the wrong moment and precipitated misunderstanding. We reached the top of the landing to find a big, dark-complexioned Arab standing ready to welcome me. He was wearing beautiful robes of black silk, and had a white handkerchief thrown back over his head. Hanging from his neck, almost down to his waist, was a very striking chain of ivory prayer beads. He was a tall man of well over six feet, and very heavily built. His features were heavy, but relieved by a high forehead. His flowing Arabic and cultured conversation set me at ease at once.

GETTING IN TOUCH

He explained that he was entirely friendly to our cause, but that he had asked me to visit him at night because he had many fanatics in the town, and wished to ensure that no untoward incident should occur. Coffee was served in a set of excellent French china, by the side of which the clumsy coffee-flask of Arab pottery looked very incongruous. Coffee is always poured out of a well-seasoned flask, for it is then at its best, just as a well-seasoned earthen teapot is considered best for a brew of tea.

Among some tribes in Iraq and in Northern Arabia it is considered good manners to accept three cups of coffee. It is said that the second cup is the dangerous one, for the host will give the first cup in welcome, while, if he intends treachery, he will insert a pinch of arsenic into the guest's second cup. Other poisons are sometimes used, which act so quickly that the host does not need to offer a third cup. The third cup is therefore considered somewhat as a seal of friendship. This Borgia-like practice is now seldom resorted to, though I must own that on one occasion I considered it advisable to make an excuse after the second cup, exit hurriedly and put my fingers down my throat.

On this present occasion I was surprised at the large size of the cups of coffee which were served, and found it heavy work drinking the first two cups somewhat hurriedly, so as to ask for a third one, which was promptly served. On a later occasion, when I knew Seyidt Mahomedt bin Idrissi intimately, I told him about this inconvenience. We laughed heartily when he assured me that the three-cup system was not known in his lands, and he had been amused to find that I was such a thirsty guest.

When the third cup had been served I felt at ease, and we talked smoothly on political and other subjects. With wireless telegrams always to hand, and many confidential reports at my fingers-ends, I expected to find that I was better versed in Middle Eastern politics than this bedou chief of an almost unknown Arabian district. I soon learned that I was talking like a child to an expert, and told Seyidt Mahomedt that I did not know enough about the subject to argue with him.

He smiled pleasantly, and turned easily to a discussion of geography. Here, again, I felt that I should surely find I had superior knowledge, for my profession had taken me afar, and, from a Western point of view, I was by no means ignorant of general geography. Within a few minutes we were discussing Middle Eastern states, and I found the Seyidt carried the map of Europe in his mind in a way that very few Europeans could boast of. After an hour or two of polite conversation we started on the real business in hand.

"Seyidt Mahomedt," I said finally, "I know nothing about Arab politics, and I am not going to pretend that I do. You can tell me anything you like, and I shall never be in the position to contradict you. It is only the result that will count."

GETTING IN TOUCH

On this note the interview terminated, and the future proved that the Seyidt was a man of his word. So long as matters were conducted on a frank and honest basis, my relations with Seyidt Mahomedt bin Idrissi were satisfactory, for he was an honest man, and also a very shrewd one, and when I insisted on driving a bargain he always got the better of it.

For a time I had set aside all thoughts of my private quest for Ophir, but in a curious manner it obtruded itself once more, and on this occasion I encountered for the first time the Gold of Ophir.

For political reasons I used to take many a sheikh on a sea voyage. One of my guests seemed rather seasick and homesick, and, as we were nearing the harbour, I tried to rouse him to conversation, so that he might forget his woes.

" What are you complaining about, sheikh?" I said. " Here you have the rolling seas, the bracing winds, and all that man may desire. Ashore you have nothing but flies, fleas, and sand."

The sheikh was very indignant. His lands held everything. Yes, he would prove it. What would I like? A bag of gold?

I laughingly agreed, and as we were entering harbour suggested a cup of coffee might be more welcome for the present. I often wish now that we had exchanged visiting-cards, for during the next month I forgot my friend's address. But a few days later a canoe hailed us.

TREASURE OF OPHIR

"*Ho Quabtan.* Ho, Captain, stop your ship."

We lowered a ladder, and a fisherman, a poverty-stricken fellow, climbed up the gangway with a sack over his shoulder.

"What have you got there, Kalil?" I asked.

He dumped the sack down with a grunt.

"Thank God that job's over. What have I brought? I don't know. The sheikh said it was a bag of gold. See for yourself."

We were in somewhat narrow coral waters just then, and by the time I had tended to the safety of the ship Kalil and his canoe had disappeared. I opened the bag, to find that it was a bag of gold all right, rich, alluvial gold sand!

Evidently my recent guest was not only keeping a jesting promise, but he was also inviting me to develop his property. I have located the Gold of Ophir three times, but always in inaccessible places. If however, I could discover that lost sheikh, the world should re-enjoy some of that treasure without any further delay.

CHAPTER VI

ON THE RIGHT TRACK

EVERY man of this generation knows that war work is hard work, and holds but little romance. I realized that I must put away all my private ambitions for discovering Ophir. Yet the kindly Fates decreed otherwise. Came a day when our ship was refitting at Bombay, and the Commander-in-Chief sent for me.

"You will finish your refitting, and then return to your patrol station. A lighter bound for Basra has been lost and information suggests that the crew has been saved by the Arabs of Masirah Islands. Use your knowledge and search the coast as necessary."

The Admiral waited to hear if his orders were quite clear, while I made some rapid calculations regarding coal consumption and suchlike technicalities. Everything was clear and in order, so I saluted and withdrew.

I realized that a great deal would depend on what information we gained at Masirah Island, and if nothing definite was learned there I decided to search the coast to southward, for such experience as I had gained of that little-known coast suggested that the more habitable and better-watered shores lay to southward. If the men were on the coast at all I expected to find them to the south rather than to the north. The lost land of Ophir might possibly lie in that direction, but it is only fair to add that I did not allow such an interesting consideration to bias an endeavour to search for seamen in distress.

We reached Masirah in due course, but could learn nothing from the natives there. The Arabs are a very secretive race, though if you can get on the right side of an Arab and make him talkative, he will let slip all the information he possesses. At Masirah the natives had looted the shipwrecked lighter, and they could, if they had chosen, have given us all the information we required. They were, however, afraid we had come to punish them for looting.

This was unfortunate, for if I had known those simple facts, I should have praised them for their endeavours to save the lighter, overlooked any petty looting, and given them some small reward for services rendered. Past experience convinces me that they would have given us all information, and used their best endeavours on our behalf. From the Islands we approached the mainland, and found a desolate, waterless coast. We knew of no water to northward, and therefore promptly commenced our search to southward. There we were wrong.

Some of the Masirah Arabs had already come in contact with the Europeans of Aden, and wished to

ON THE RIGHT TRACK

protect these British castaways, but directly they saw the looting commence they were afraid that the British sailors might be roughly handled, and so they took charge of the crew, and hurried them from the scene. Later, fearing some of the wilder spirits of the looting crowd might act on the maxim that "dead men tell no tales", they put our crew aboard a small fishing boat, took them to the mainland, and hurried them along the coast. One of the survivors later told me the tale.

The seamen had a very anxious time of it, for they could speak no Arabic, and expected to be knifed any moment. At the best they hoped they would be sold into slavery, and possibly find a chance to escape. They were barefooted, and the burning sun of midday blistered their feet. They were given very little water, and practically no food. Yet in truth the Arabs were doing their best for them, hurrying them over desert stretches while the food lasted and water held out. The Arabs well knew that a European requires a tremendous amount of water in comparison with the needs of the native born.

At length they reached a small river that is not known to European geography, and from there a small boat was obtained in which they coasted to the nearest dhow port. Here they were transhipped to a dhow of moderate size, on which they were more comfortable, and they finally worked round the coast to Muscat. It is pleasant to add that the British political officer

TREASURE OF OPHIR

promptly rewarded the Arabs with many thanks and liberal payment.

Meanwhile we headed our ship southward, and made careful search of the coast. We knew that if the shipwrecked crew were still alive and anywhere on the coast, a few rags would be waved to attract our attention. In uncharted waters, feeling her way with the lead, our little ship nosed herself into many a small fishing anchorage, where no steamship had yet been seen, but we saw no sign of the shipwrecked crew. Meanwhile the Engineer Commander had been making careful calculations, and found we had reached the safety margin of his coal consumption. It was necessary to give up this coasting, and make straight for Aden by the deep water track.

By now we had reached the water-bearing coasts, and could feel fairly well assured that if our friends had worked further southward they had not died of thirst. The anticipated Ophir lands lay at least two days further south, but we had to keep out in deep water some two miles too distant to observe the coast. I judged I had come nearer to the goal of my dreams than at any other period of my investigations, but, after twenty-five years of search for Ophir, I was obliged to head to sea again, murmuring "so near and yet so far".

There was hard work on hand, with cares and attendant anxieties, and after months of monotonous patrol for the ship's company and more interesting political work for myself, we returned to Aden for a short spell

ON THE RIGHT TRACK

and for the cleaning of our boilers. As we lay at anchor, officers and men planning recreation for the rare two days ashore in a civilized seaport, a boatload of visitors approached, friends from the little British colony of Somaliland, and we eagerly brought out our telescopes to see if our own particular chums were in the boat.

In those days practically every Englishman abroad was wearing the King's uniform, but in this boat was a civilian, a man who was evidently of combatant age. My interest was aroused, and I asked myself what service, if any, he could be doing for his country which did not entitle him to wear uniform? It was no idle curiosity on my part, for I had charge of a long coastline, all along which there were intrigues, as there were everywhere else in the world. It was plainly my duty to know all about this gentleman's activities.

I stayed at the gangway to welcome our guests, and was introduced to Mr. Murreyl.

" How do you do?" I said. " I don't think we have met before. Which way are you bound?"

Murreyl's eyes twinkled.

" I am going to Merbat," he said, and his manner conveyed the suggestion: " I bet you don't know where that is."

" Oh, yes?" I replied vaguely, and faded off before the conversation developed further.

Merbat! I knew perfectly where Merbat was, for it was on my coastal patrol. Not very far from Merbat

TREASURE OF OPHIR

I had met with a small adventure, and had been quite glad to return to the ship with a whole skin.

"Secret service, presumably," I mused. "But it is curious that intelligence reports have given me no warning."

I sent for the files, and ran rapidly through them, but there was nothing about Mr. Murreyl under his own name or any pseudonym. I felt really puzzled. It began to look as if Mr. Murreyl was not an Englishman, and I could see no reason to accept his statement about Merbat.

There were no known intrigues or enemy activities anywhere near Merbat, and if he went there he would be pretty well isolated, for Ras Merbat is the eastern extremity of the small Dhofar district, a nice little oasis, but somewhat off the map. However, I could very rapidly take the necessary steps to ensure that he did not leave Aden, either by ship or by shore-boat, until he had proved his *bona fides,* and in the meantime he was my guest until I had perfected those precautions.

I asked him to luncheon, and during that meal I chattered blandly, telling only the truth and being careful to show what an absolute ass I could be. Confidence begets confidence, and no man minds capping the yarns of a garrulous fool, but I failed to draw Murreyl, and decided that he was either too clever to be drawn by me, or that he had nothing on his mind worth my attention.

That was my summary after half an hour of hard

ON THE RIGHT TRACK

work and complete exhaustion of conversational effort. When at last Murreyl spoke, he merely repeated his assertion that he was going to Merbat, and asked if I could advise him as to the best way to get there.

This time I felt constrained to believe him.

" I should like to shake hands with you, Murreyl," I answered at length, " for I think you are the bravest man I have ever met."

Murreyl gasped with surprise. " What do you mean? I don't understand!" he exclaimed.

" Have a cigar. Let us go into the matter quietly," I suggested, leaning back in my chair with rather over-studied ease. " You suggest going to Merbat, knowing nothing of the coast, none of the tribes, and not a word of Arabic. Perhaps there is no harm done there, for in our work we often find that a little knowledge is a dangerous thing. But I should like to know *why* you want to go to Merbat."

He then told me that a French explorer had come to London with stories of vast grain stores hidden near Merbat. Murreyl's scheme was simply to go there and buy up the grain for cash. The mystery that I had been weaving round him thus had a very simple explanation, but I felt I ought to point out to him some of the difficulties he might meet with.

It is, for instance, usually considered unwise to exhibit a bag of gold to a bedou people, unless you have the necessary introductions which will enable you to ensure that the tribe shall behave with courtesy and discretion. I hold a theory that a man is inviolable so long as he is fearless, though, alas! I have so many white feathers that I have been unable to test the theory to my satisfaction, and Murreyl was not overkeen to try it out for me.

When I had explained the difficulties more fully, he realized that his proposition seemed impracticable, and decided to abandon it if something more suitable were available.

I suggested Abyssinia as being a land with great resources, most of which are undeveloped, whilst many are unmarketed. Murreyl decided to tackle the grain stores of Abyssinia, whilst on my part I promised to get him some useful introductions there.

"I rather wanted to go to Ras Merbat," he sighed. "They say there is an old place called Ophir thereabouts. Have you ever heard of it?"

I was interested, but not particularly thrilled by this information. True, he was suggesting the exact place where I expected to find Ophir; but on the other hand there were so many pseudo-Ophirs which I had already visited, that I felt some reserve in accepting any untried theories.

When Murreyl left he gave me a copy of Professor Kean's "Gold of Ophir", which contains an excellent summary of the work of former investigators and many a useful hint with which to establish the true identity of Ophir. I merely dipped into the book, and did not study it, since I wished to approach the subject with an

Makalla [Facing page 91

ON THE RIGHT TRACK

open mind and without leaning too heavily on greater authorities; but before long I was again poring over my charts and notes.

In wartime I had no right to go joy-riding to the Dhofar district unless the trip was entirely justifiable and in accord with Government interests. But grain was becoming valuable, and if I found a hidden store of vast dimensions I should be finding a very valuable treasure. Evidence showed that the Dhofar district might well produce more grain than it could consume, but the real problem might lie in finding how to get the stuff away. There are many treasures in little-known parts of the world, well located, but untouched, and fortunes await the proper development of transport, and especially inter-port transport.

My charts showed me promising harbours, and I knew how to organize the camel transport and dhow service, so that I felt I should be fully justified in taking a trip to Ras Merbat and the Dhofar district, but the first practical step was a visit to the Sultan of Makalla. If there were any large grain stores near to Merbat, the Sultan would probably know something of them. If the idea was worth developing, Makalla would become the main shipping port.

What was the road like from Makalla to Merbat?

How many camels were available?

Those were two most important questions, for undoubtedly Makalla was the key to the situation.

TREASURE OF OPHIR

We timed our navigation so as to arrive at daybreak.

Makalla is a picturesque little town, built at the foot of some steep hills. The Sultan, using Indian experience, has developed his port, so that it is one of the best shipping harbours of the Arabian coast. It is sheltered from the north monsoon, but during the south monsoon another portion of the bay has to be used. The sea was dead calm and in the morning stillness there was not a breath of air to ripple the ocean surface. As the ship steamed toward the shore the cry of the *muezzin* echoed over the water. "God is the Greatest" came their cry.

" No bottom," cried the leadsman, as the wet line went hissing through his hands.

" Come to prayer," urged the *muezzin* from the mosque.

" Four-r-teen fathoms," called the leadsman.

The anchor plunged, and the cable roared through the hawsepipe with desecrating rattle.

" Come to success," urged the *muezzin* in final appeal.

" Lower away," cried the officer of the watch, and the gangway creaked down to its resting-place. An Arab boat came alongside, and an Arab gentleman climbed aboard, full of his own importance.

" Hold on a minute," laughed the officer of the watch, and clutched the visitor by his cotton skirt, which came off.

ON THE RIGHT TRACK

"Don't do that," exclaimed the Arab, in excellent English. "I am the Port Admiral."

This sort of thing was rather astonishing when we thought we were three hundred miles from nowhere. But Makalla had a smarter service than you will meet with at many a European port.

The Port Admiral came up and saluted me.

"What time would you like to visit His Highness the Sultan? Any time will be convenient, for His Highness starts work at sunrise. Would you like the carriage or the motor-car?" he queried. "Shall I stay here, or will you find your own way to the shore? Oh, yes. I shall be there to meet you. Good morning."

The motor-car was a good one, and the drive was amusing. There was a bargeing match with a camel, but the car won and delivered me at the palace in comfort. His Highness welcomed his English guest in a drawing-room that was furnished with the quaintest mixture of Europe and the East. There were bookcases of beautiful Indian carving, and a table of Burmese work, but the chairs were European and their upholstery was very worn. On the side cases there were beautiful examples of Indian and Chinese ivory carvings, and by their side was a plaster model of a coach-and-four, in which one of the leaders had lost his off foreleg, so that the model was more fit for the dustbin than for the State-room of an Eastern Sultan.

His Highness had a collection of stones spread on his table. There was some copper ore, one or two specimens of rock with sulphur in them, something that had the appearance of silver ore, and a piece of lignite that looked like coal.

"What do you think of them?" asked the Sultan, fingering his geological collection.

But I was not going to give opinions on a subject on which I was not qualified to speak.

"If you think your land holds minerals, why don't you send to Aden?" I suggested.

"Well, I did send them a letter," the Sultan answered.

"How long ago?"

"Oh, about nineteen years, but I have forgotten the exact date of the month."

He was rather a patient man, and he was still awaiting the answer, which he hoped I had brought. He listened to the theories about Merbat and its hidden grain stores, but said that he did not know much about such matters. However, he would send for the captains of dhows and for travellers who had visited those lands, and let me know the result of his inquiries by evening. He asked the officers of the ship to dinner, and suggested that we should discuss all information then.

The dinner was a good one, and interesting for the first fifteen courses. It dragged a little after that, and came to an abrupt conclusion at the end of the twenty-third course, at which some of the Arab guests seemed disappointed, though the ship's officers, true to naval discipline, bore up bravely. There was not much

ON THE RIGHT TRACK

information about Merbat, but what there was proved valuable, so we set sail for Dhofar, and again timed the navigation so as to reach there by sunrise.

Shortly after dawn the navigator sighted the white house that was our definite landmark, and there too, was the palm fringe showing dark against the light foreshore. Further to north lay the headland of Ras Merbat, and half-way between the white house and Merbat lay. . . ? If Ophir did not lie there, I should have to build up my theories again, and find some different method of deduction.

With the rising sun the swell of the Indian Ocean came rolling in from eastward, and a dull booming told us seamen that no ship's boat could live in the heavy surf that was breaking ashore. If no surf-boat came from the shore, then landing would be impracticable. But when you have worked through the night to meet disappointment in the morning, there is nothing like a good breakfast.

A knock at the cabin door heralded the officer of the watch, who reported that a shore-boat was approaching, and that she was the quaintest-looking craft he had ever seen. With my mouth full of buttered toast I mumbled my thanks, and came out of the cabin to welcome the approaching visitors.

The boat certainly was a quaint craft, for her frame was made of bent boughs, mostly of gum incense wood. Her hull was of untanned ox hides sewn with leather laces, and she leaked plentifully at every seam. In the

TREASURE OF OPHIR

stern sheets stood the village patriarch, chanting a psalm to keep the rowers in time. He would sing one line, and if they knew it the crew would sing the next line in answer. If they didn't they just sang " La, la, la ".

It all sounds very beautiful when first you hear this boat chant; but when you are able to follow the words it is also amusing. Usually the verse is extempore, in which case the crew repeat each line, and if it is the local village song it seldom gets beyond the first verse. Here is a typical chant :

> " Ali's a fool,"
> " Not so fast,"
> " You keep cool,"
> " Dam and blast."

On one occasion a boat's crew took me five miles to a monotonous refrain of which the only words were "There's a girl across the river. And her face is like a peach."

Perhaps the present chanty was more dignified, because it appertained to the State barge, containing the local aristocracy all dressed up for the occasion. Arrived at the gangway, Sheikh Abdulla climbed aboard with with some difficulty for the village sword was too tightly girt, and he was not used to sandals. He was, however, blessed with common sense and a vein of humour. He stumbled about five steps up the ship's

ON THE RIGHT TRACK

ladder, and then took off his sandals and threw them down into the boat. With a well-directed shot he hit slave Omar on the head with the second sandal, and before he got to the top of the gangway he unbuckled his sword and passed that down, too. I began to like Abdulla before we had shaken hands.

His brother, Sheikh Nasr, followed, and then the whole boat's crew decided they might as well have a look at the ship. They all came to our State cabin where coffee was served, and Sheikh Nasr was so talkative that no one else got a word in, until Francis the Goanese steward settled the matter. He opened a tin of mixed biscuits, and gave a sugar-topped one to each of the guests, but to Sheikh Nasr he awarded a large dry cracknel.

" Eat it whole," he whispered, in Arabic.

The rest of Nasr's endless anecdote was lost in a cloud of flour and a fit of coughing.

The whole joyous crowd came sight-seeing, but they were difficult to entertain, for the wireless roused no wonder and the electric fan left them cold. Sheikh Nasr saved the situation by asking for a glass of water. Someone went to the drinking fountain and turned on the tap. Here was a wonder indeed! Water by merely twiddling your fingers instead of drawing it from the well. By the time they had finished playing with the fountain, the whole wardroom was flooded.

The First Lieutenant came ashore with me to return the sheikh's call and a happy crowd met us, all armed to the teeth. Evidently they were peaceful folk, for their armoury was quaint. Some had old rifles, others spears, and these together with a few bludgeons and a couple of billhooks completed the weapons of the sheikh's guard of honour by which we were escorted to the sheikh's house where we were received by a courteous host.

After the formalities we settled down to business. I praised the crops, though as a matter of fact I had not seen them.

"Yes," the sheikh agreed, "the harvest promised well this year."

I then asked him the price of grain and he gave me his quotation.

"Ah, yes," I parried, "that is the price per sack, but we require several thousand camel loads."

The sheikh shook his head and explained that they only grew enough for their immediate needs. They had plenty of land and could grow an unlimited quantity, but prosperity would only invite the raiding bedou. A quiet life was better than all the storms of commerce and the disturbance of bedou raids. There was peace and plenty and that was sufficient for these Sons of Joktan. There was no large harvest and no hidden grain stores of vast supplies in the hills, so there was the answer to my ambitions for relieving the grain shortage.

"Where is the City of Ophir?" I asked, suddenly. The sheikh looked puzzled. "Where is the City of

ON THE RIGHT TRACK

Dhofar?" I amended, but the inquiry sounded much the same.

"Oh! Al Bilad, The City," answered our host. "Do you want to go to it? Abdulla will take you," and an hour later we set forth.

The road led through a coconut grove and then onward through more open country. We passed several fields of jowari, the native millet which is the staple grain of the country. All the fields were well irrigated and we two visitors pretended we were very thirsty for we wished to examine the wells, in a land where water is wealth. The coconut groves had already told us that water was abundant and close to the surface, for the coconut palm only thrives where there is plenty of moisture and as its tap root goes down about nine feet we knew that there was water at that depth. By tasting the water from several wells we found that all the streams were sweet and came from the hills to north of us, so we came to the conclusion that this land was capable of supporting a large population.

This also satisfied an essential query regarding the possibility of it being the Land of Ophir. I had already noted the neighbouring harbours and was satisfied that there was sufficient safe accommodation for the native dhows. But I was not ready to accept as Ophir a ruined city, however large, unless it could also show a harbour; and I saw little to lead me to expect to find a hidden harbour on this iron-bound coast.

Then we sighted the ruins, and before we reached

TREASURE OF OPHIR

them the position became clear to me. This town possessed something extremely rare on Arab sea-coasts, namely, a small river running to a sea outlet.

In many parts of Arabia you will find small streams, or perhaps river beds, that are in flood for a portion of the year, but they seldom have a sea outlet. This river was only a tiny stream from a European point of view, but its existence and its position were of the utmost importance to the Ophir problem. I carefully examined the stream before giving any attention to the ruins, for my archæological knowledge is negligible, but here I was tackling a subject on which I had professional knowledge. A khor or ravine gave natural wharfage to the seaport, but a thin ribbon of coral sand had drawn across the harbour mouth and strangled the prosperity of the City.

The ruins proved very interesting and I formed certain conclusions about them. Even if they represent Ophir they may well have been rebuilt many times, for that is the custom in Arabia, where a town is inhabited by a fresh generation when the ground site has been dried and cleansed by the Arabian sun.

The problem was not so interesting to my companion, who wandered back to the stream, for to those who have been months without sight of fresh water a hill stream holds peculiar fascination. I wandered down to the sea and on the outskirts of the ruins sat down, listening to the roar of the surf and inhaling deep draughts of pure content, for I was convinced that I

ON THE RIGHT TRACK

had found Ophir, the City for which I had searched from childhood until I was a man, almost of middle age.

I saw no object in delaying the publication of my discovery, but after I had sat for some time Reason came to my rescue and relentlessly paraded the facts before me. A minor excavation by the citadel stood silent witness, probably to the work of Theodore Bent who lost his life while on a visit to South Arabia, and I began to realize that men have made the study of Ophir a life's work and yet failed to bring conviction to the public.

I had done so little while others had done so much, and I realized that ancient Ophir required no half-hearted service, for a nation's prosperity might be founded by its reawakening. Either I must be prepared to study and arrange my proofs until they became entirely convincing, or I should leave the work in better hands. I could take my choice of the Navy or the development of Ophir, but meanwhile there was a war on, and everything else must wait.

CHAPTER VII

WAITING

When I assembled my proofs I could see, still more clearly, why I should wait.

The City of Ophir was found but that was not sufficient. Ophir was the name of a land inhabited by the Ophir tribe and the City was but the main seaport of that tribe. The Gold of Ophir was one of the treasures exported from that land.

I must identify the Land of Ophir, the City of Ophir, and the Gold of Ophir, so that when the time is ripe the Land shall prosper, the City shall reawaken, and the Gold shall render self-supporting the whole of Arabia.

So far I had seen the City but had only touched the fringes of the Land and had not properly located the Gold. I saw further the necessity of wresting from obscurity the story of the former ruler of the Land, Bilkis the Beautiful, Queen of Sheba, and of her romance with Suleiman the Wise whose kingdom she planned to unite with her own. In that story I might find further proofs to substantiate my discoveries and also perchance to awaken a romance which may prove of world-wide interest.

The Temple of Ophir

[*Facing page* 102

WAITING

In far-off mosques in little known lands, on Arab house-tops under the silver Arabian moon, my Arab friends have gathered for me historical facts that I may show to the West. Those who are better qualified than I can dress the dry bones of history and set forth a romance that lives bright and unstained through its sleep of ages; the story of how the wisest man in the world wooed, won, and lost the most beautiful woman of the land; the story of how a queen gave her throne for the love of her people, while she offered to Suleiman the sure foundations of prosperity for two empires. That story I should be able to show to the world if I could but uncover the facts that lay buried in the hinterland.

.   .   .   .   .

"To the man who can wait all doors will ultimately open," says the Chinese proverb, and I waited awhile until I had the opportunity of retiring from the Navy with such gratuity as I had earned. Then once again I travelled to Arabia, to spend many years in the Tihima, those desert lands which the Arabs call "the place of heat".

Sometimes I have lived at ease, the guest of Arab princes, but I have also frequently lived as a simple bedou. Thus I have had the opportunity of observing all grades of Arabian society.

An Arabian prince of the Tihima leads a very busy life. He rises shortly before sunrise, bathes, dresses, and then with the rising sun he obeys the call of the *muezzin*. On the house-top of a Prince's guest-house I would sleep lightly and was usually awake before the break of day, and as the morning lightened, a thin wavering call would break the silence of dawn, strengthening as the *muezzin* found his voice. These keepers of the mosques are usually men frail of body, and in the evening of life, but they are strong of voice, for their duties include calling the faithful to prayer.

That call to prayer was far more persuasive than the soulless clank of a western church bell. I would watch the *muezzin* on the tower balcony turning to each quarter of the horizon, singing his sweet chant while he raised his hands to his ears in token that the voice of Heaven bade the Faithful answer his summons. Then the prince and a few followers would come to the mosque, passing close by my house. After the morning service he would take a short walk and often cut short his hour of leisure to pay a call on his European guest. The rest of his day and far into the night would be spent on the administrative work of the country and on the entertainment of visiting sultans, sherriffs, seyidts, and sheikhs.

The Arab aristocracy have few titles and do not use them in Western style. "Sultan" is really a Turkish title but it has been introduced into Arabia, and specially into the land where Turkish control was fairly effective. A sultan is a ruler, but most of the Arab sultans are

WAITING

only rulers of petty principalities. Sherriff is a Northern title and is practically equivalent to Duke.

The seyidts are the descendants of the Prophet Mahomedt, and are in general a ruling class. The Seyidts of Assir have given me many years of hospitality. There are many minor seyidts, and on one occasion I found a seyidt who was very glad to be my personal servant. The poor fellow was very grateful to find that a Christian fully appreciated his Moslem title. Sheikh is a word which denotes that the man is sprung from the leading family of his tribe, and the title is so common that it is an equivalent to Squire of English speech. We have the Sultan of Shukra, quite a small principality, the Sherriff of Behain, a district quite as important as Shukra, and we have sheikhs of every village.

Whilst seyidts, sultans, sherriffs, and sheikhs have welcomed me with their open-handed hospitality, I have at times, as I have said, lived as a bedou. I have never ranged the desert in fierce bedou raids, though I have frequently assisted in repulsing those raids. Here let me digress to say that the Arab outlook toward raiding is very different to that of the European. The raider is not regarded as a mere robber, on a par with a burglar, but as a sportsman pursuing a sporting venture and taking the full risks of his sport. Mine was the more humble life of a working bedou, who is thankful to earn his daily bread and find shelter from the sun during the noon-day heat.

TREASURE OF OPHIR

My savings dwindled until one day I sat in my Arab office watching a hunting spider working for his breakfast; I myself had no work and soon I should have no breakfast. I watched the little fellow stalking warily, for he builds no web and his livelihood depends on his agility. Again and again he missed his quarry. My observations were interrupted by a knock on the door, and there entered the cicerone who usually accompanied me on my expeditions.

"Hullo, Saleh," I cried. "Have a cigarette? No, you prefer a cigar, I remember," thankful I had some Indian cheroots to offer. Saleh took a chair and got to business.

"The Sultan has dreamed a dream!" He paused impressively. "The Prophet Mahomedt, on whose name be peace, came to him saying: 'Dig here and you will find silver, dig there and you will find gold.'"

Saleh's story ended as abruptly as it began and I was left to make my own inferences. Of course, the Sultan had not sent forty miles merely for the pleasure of boasting about an interesting dream. For some reason he did not wish to be explicit, though in all probability Saleh knew more about the matter.

"Very well, Saleh, how soon can we start?" I asked.

We had a forty-mile motor drive, along a sand beach where there was not a single pebble. Our luggage was simple for it mainly consisted of Saleh's magnificent water-pipe and its seven feet of flexible mouthpiece. We chose the next low tide, and at daybreak we passed the

WAITING

Aden wireless station and headed eastward with thousands of small crabs scuttling across our path.

We passed a few east-bound caravans, and many caravans bound from the east for Aden. Then as the sun rose, the mirage commenced. Some great Djinn would appear ahead, wavy and indistinct. Then as our car snorted up to this apparition it would form into a bedou asleep on his camel, for he had been riding through the night. At last we got to our rendezvous where we expected to find the Sultan's guard awaiting for us, but unfortunately they had turned up forty-eight hours too soon and had gone away again.

Saleh did not know his way to the palace, so we waited under a *tenta*, a small sun-roof which was supported by three poles. The Sultan's cousin, Sultan Kamal, had a seaside hut nearby, and he sent a welcome to us. His hut was a typical one, with light poles and canes for uprights, grass matting and thatch roof. Inside was a sand floor, well carpeted with grass mats. This type of hut makes a very cool and comfortable dwelling place, though the thatch roof soon harbours mice. To combat the mice there are always plenty of cats, but as the cats are inveterate thieves they are almost as much of a nuisance as the mice would be.

Sultan Kamal gave us coffee and launched into his woes. He had bought a new suit and a new turban, and very nice they appeared to be. Unfortunately the clothes were overloaded with indigo dye, and when the Sultan perspired, his face and body became plentifully coloured with the surplus indigo. It is a very common mishap and I don't think that the Sultan would have minded, but for the unexpected visitor. He was very keen to be on good terms with the Aden Authorities, and when the first European visitor turned up he was in the blues, literally—and all over!

"You see, this suit is a very good one really. In fact, it is brand new, and I put it on to welcome you," he explained. "But please understand that I do not usually walk about with a blue face."

In truth I fully appreciated his predicament, for if he had washed his face with native soap while the indigo was still fresh, he would only have increased his troubles. You cannot well offer your royal host a cake of carbolic soap the first time you meet him, even if his face is dirty. Instead I tried to sympathize and only made matters worse. I told him I thought it suited him very well, but he feared I would consider him a blue-stained bedou, one who smears himself liberally with indigo and henna.

I tried to change the subject, and asked if he had heard about his cousin's dream.

"I don't know anything about that," he answered, "but look at my hands!"

Then a bright idea struck him. He would show me that he was not really the bedou he appeared to be, so he took off his coat, ostensibly to show me its texture. This left him bare to the waist, a very common state of *deshabille* in the Tihima summer-time, but luck was

WAITING

against him, for the coat was as overloaded with dye as the turban.

"Oh, Allah!" he wailed. "My body is as blue as my face!"

Here I made another mistake in not allowing fair play to natural instincts, and howling with laughter; for now that I know Sultan Kamal well I am certain that he would have joined in. However, you do not laugh at a distressed host the first time he entertains you. Fortunately the camels arrived from the palace before long and in mounting I contrived to fall off—by-mistake-on-purpose, and so we parted in jest instead of in sorrow.

By the time we reached the Sultan's palace it was sunset. The Sultan was standing at his doorstep, a young man of about thirty, very simply dressed. He was wearing a blue turban with a bunch of fresh date blossom in it, and a light-blue cotton coat which was open, showing a good chest and rippling stomach muscles. Round his middle was a short blue cotton petticoat, girt with a djambieh, the curved dagger that is worn in front. His legs were bare, and he was wearing no sandals.

"In my own country I greet you in my own clothes," he remarked.

I had seen him at Aden, all dolled up with silken turban, flowing robes, jewelled embroidered sandals, and reeking with Indian perfume, but I liked him better in his own setting, for it made him look the man that

TREASURE OF OPHIR

he was. I told him so, much to Saleh's annoyance, for Saleh explained afterwards that he had great difficulty in persuading the Sultan to put on his "Sunday Bests" when going to pay an official call at Aden Residency.

The Sultan took us to the roof, and there the evening meal was served, but first we were given hot milk, well sweetened. This was very refreshing and served us well until the evening meal was ready. The Sultan explained that they had slain a kid for us, but as we had turned up late it had all been eaten. However, we had not long to wait, and in the meantime the Sultan showed us the surrounding country till fading twilight blotted out our house-top panorama.

I did not ask the Sultan anything about his dream, for I knew that he was burning to show me his discoveries. The meal was an excellent one, the stewed lamb was done to a nicety, and the lamb's head was served in the approved style to show that we had not been entertained merely with a joint. There was breadfruit stuffed with rice and mince, braised chicken, fried kabobs seasoned with fresh-pounded chillies, fresh-cooked flapjack bread all crisp and hot, and lastly shortcake soaked in date honey. Be careful when you meet that last dish. Honey from bees whose hives are near date palms is luscious, but has strong laxative effects.

After dinner we settled down to business. First the Sultan told me that second sight was in his family. His grandfather, when ruling Sultan, had a dream showing a bedou sheikh who was coming to meet him with

WAITING

intent to assassinate him. The dream was a very clear one and the Sultan had particularly noted the dress of the sheikh, who carried a knife concealed under his cloak. When a few days later the sheikh himself approached he was recognized by his dress and immediately arrested. He then confessed that he had intended to throw the knife at the Sultan. The Sultan asked what his grievance was and gave him redress for it. He also forgave him for his intent to murder, for he felt that as he had been warned by a dream the matter had been taken out his hands.

I expressed suitable appreciation of the story and assured the Sultan that such dreams were not unknown to Western peoples. He then told me his own dream and asked me for an immediate interpretation. Now I had already analysed that dream and realized that if it was a true one it had certainly been tested and the Sultan had found something before sending for me. Perhaps he had found some cache of gold and silver coins and wanted me to dispose of them at a fair price. But the question that surged uppermost in my thoughts was as to whether he had found the Gold of Ophir, and if so in what form? " Gold and Silver," said the dream.

I could see he had something up his sleeve, so I acted up to my old principles and asked no questions. There was a pause, with a contest of wills. The Sultan looked to see if I would laugh; then finding I kept a grave face he apparently felt encouraged to assume that I would investigate the problem properly, and further, seemed to assume that as I had shown no hasty keenness I was not over avaricious.

"Here is the gold," he whispered, untying a canvas bag.

I dipped my hand into a pile of sand and let it go dribbling through my fingers. Under the moonlight, the sand glittered and showed that there was apparently metal in it, but that was all I could say for certain.

"What do you think of it?" he asked.

"Well, Sultan, I may tell you more in the morning," I answered cautiously, for I had the uneasy feeling that though I might be able to tell gold when ready coined I was not quite so sure when it was in any other form. Fortunately I had recently looked up a text-book and I eagerly poured out my new-found knowledge. I explained that there were two kinds of gold known to Europeans.

"There is the true gold, Sultan, and there is Fool's Gold," I said.

"I think that Fool's Gold is what the Sultan has found," came a voice from the night. The Wazir was not going to be left out of this conversation and had silently joined us.

I took a handful and panned it out, in the fashion that Mr. G. A. Henty described in one of the thrilling novels of my boyhood, but it did not work out according to programme. I swilled it around, fast and slow, violently and gently, but the glittering substance would not separate from the sand. This was not

WAITING

gold, nor was it the common Fool's Gold, better known as iron pyrites.

I was frankly puzzled and making my excuses, I bade the Sultan good night and sought my bed. As soon as it was dawn I took a walk into the country, taking my problem with me. I picked up a few stones of the country together with a handful of sand and a piece of hornblend, and put them in my pocket. As I walked my problem was solved for me, for when a little later I put my hand to my pocket I drew it out full of glittering sand, such as the Sultan had shown to me. The hornblend had powdered and mixed with the desert sand.

The problem was solved, but there was a more interesting one awaiting me, for now I knew that the sand he had shown me had little to do with the Sultan's dream, since he certainly had not found it where the dream told him to dig. But directly I reached the palace he asked me for my judgment on his gold sand.

"Why waste time, Sultan?" I replied. "The Holy Prophet, blessings on his name, bade you dig for your gold and silver. You have not dug for this sand. Take it back, it is worthless."

The Sultan's grandfather, an old man of one hundred and thirteen years, called me aside. He was very blind but he was active-brained.

"Craufurd, do you think the dream is true?" he asked; to which I gave a non-committal answer.

"Would it not be better if you found the gold and

TREASURE OF OPHIR

silver ready coined?" he suggested. It seemed to me that he hinted at what I had already guessed.

"If we find the gold, Sultan, it shall be already coined," I promised.

We climbed our camels and rode through two miles of well-cultivated land. Then we passed a mound and came near to a large and interesting tumulus, littered with fragments of glass.

"Sultan, your people spoke to me yesterday of an emerald as large as the floor of a room. It is near to here, is it not?" I queried.

The Sultan replied in the affirmative and was very excited, begging for explanations.

Arabia was one of the earliest lands to make glass, and as glass is practically indestructible, being merely scratched if left exposed to the open, this litter gave no indication of the date of its manufacture.

"This was once a town," I explained. "There they made glass and the 'emerald' is but the crude glass of one of the glass pits."

He was very interested, for it was near to here that the dream had bade him dig. I was less interested, for the strong sun overhead had induced in me a high fever and my head was swimming. We led our camels round the tumulus and at the Sultan's bidding we stopped. In dismounting I fainted and was brought round with a douche of cold water. I made light of the matter which was easy, for I had only to explain that I had been thinking too hard, an explanation that seemed

WAITING

self-evident to the Sultan, who had not understood the evidence which showed me the glass factory and the ruins.

"Here is where I was told to dig," he explained. "Here you see is a room, but where is the gold?" I answered that if he dug through the whole tumulus he might possibly find a cache of coins. Probably he would have found some specimens of old Arabian glass which would quite likely be worth as much as any cache of coins.

So much then for the Sultan's dream—and mine. Disheartened and disappointed I returned to Aden, with the subject of my quest, the fabled Gold of Ophir, still dancing like a will-o'-the-wisp beyond my reach.

CHAPTER VIII

THE LAND OF SHEBA

AFTER working for several years in the Tihima, steadily accumulating facts, I began to feel that at last I was nearing the time when I could definitely establish the location of Ophir.

During this time I had sailed about in dhows and visited most of the possible markets from which came the ivory, apes and peacocks presented by the Queen of Sheba to King Suleiman. Sailing in these old-time craft I learned to handle them as they were sailed three thousand years ago. I also discovered a great deal of the information which lies hidden in the Old Testament from any but the initiated. For instance, I learned that there is more in the phrase "Ships of Tharshish" than any landsman can conceive. Also with local knowledge of the winds and currents I was able to trace out every stage of Hiram's three-year voyage to Ophir.

I now concluded that my evidence was complete and decided to publish my discoveries, though long acquaintance with the Ophir problem warned me that there might be many pitfalls which had not yet been anticipated.

THE LAND OF SHEBA

On returning to England, two London societies gave me every assistance in arranging my proofs and publishing the results of my researches. With all my arguments arranged and with maps and photographs to hand I placed my conclusions before a kindly London audience.

I had been able to find and invite to my lecture the most competent critics, and whilst I satisfied the majority of my audience I am afraid I did not entirely satisfy these experts. Their most effective criticism was that my arguments for the location of Ophir by my reconstruction of the voyage of Hiram's fleet would be equally applicable to any seaport of middle latitude. This observation was not entirely correct, but it was sufficiently damaging to make me realize that my proofs were not finally conclusive.

I realized that not only must I locate Ophir by the sea route, but that I must also discover and prove it by the land route. Also I decided to visit the Imam of Yemen at Sanaa, the city which Shem founded some seven thousand years ago, and which was one of the main cities of the Queen of Sheba. I wanted to go there, to peer into the old mosques, to find old manuscripts and study the history whose romance has lain hidden for some thirty centuries, and with the aid of all these things to reinforce my proofs.

Two days later I set sail for Yemen, one of the chief provinces of Bilkis, Queen of Sheba. My ship sailed on Friday the 13th May, so the auguries seemed unfavourable, and at Aden I met my first obstacles when I reported my intentions to the Aden Political Office. The Resident was most kind, but suggested he could hardly be helpful, which was not to be wondered at, for the authorities at Aden were having a dispute with the Imam of Yemen regarding the boundaries of the Aden Protectorate.

"We have just sent the Imam a very stiff letter, which practically amounts to an ultimatum," the Assistant Political Officer explained to me. "Any introductions we could give you would be the reverse of helpful."

"But I am not asking you to help me. I am only hoping that you will not hinder me," I replied, and I further explained that it has often been my custom to wander about Arabia without any European introductions. We both laughed at that, for the Political Officers were by no means ignorant of my quaint and seemingly aimless wanderings.

"Oh, we won't hinder you," the Resident exclaimed. "I only wish we could help you. But I want you clearly to understand that if you do get your head cut off you must not call on us for help."

He spoke so earnestly that I ignored the obvious retort, and solemnly assured him that I fully understood the conditions. Privately I admired his generosity in helping me with candid advice at a time when my proposals were so evidently unwelcome.

The Tanks, Aden
[Facing page 118

THE LAND OF SHEBA

"If you know Saleh Fulanin, go to see him," said the political officer, mentioning the name of the excellent cicerone who had accompanied me on many of my previous expeditions.

Without asking any further questions I sought out my old friend Saleh, and explained that I wanted to get to Sanaa. Saleh came to the rescue, assuring me that he would gain all necessary introductions at Hodeida, which is the seaport for Sanaa.

"But I am not going there by one of those beastly dhows," said Saleh, with the firmness of finality. To explain this remark I should mention the last time I took Saleh yachting, the holiday had not proved a success. This time he found a coastal steamer that would call at Hodeida, and we arrived there some thirty-six hours later. Saleh went ashore shortly after daybreak with the Chief of Police, who had come aboard on our arrival.

"Will you kindly wait aboard till we get a house ready for you," said the Chief of Police to me, which I thought was an ideal way of asking me to await permission to land.

Time dragged along on leaden feet, but I forced myself to have a good breakfast, for with a good breakfast to fortify the inner man the worst blows of Fate are lightened.

At noon the boat came with the answer and you may guess how eagerly I scanned the pencilled scrawl which said "Come along, everything is all right." In my eagerness I forgot to take my sunshade, a very useful piece of furniture in the Tihima lands.

The breeze was light and only sufficient to fill the cotton sails of our small fishing boat. I sat in the stern-sheets baking hot, while the boatmen poured out a tale of woe. It was the same old tale with the same old tailpiece—" and so the *Sahib* will undoubtedly pay us well for this journey?"

At the landing-stage a crowd had assembled to welcome the English visitor, and I met many an old friend, but in the background, as I expected, there was the inevitable opposition party, for the Arab likes his food and his gossip highly spiced.

The friendly party suggested that I had been sent out specially from England to Aden and thence to Hodeida to see if there was any possibility of restoring friendship with the Government of Yemen. The opposition party said that I was certainly a British Government Official in disguise, who had come to spy out the land before the British should deliver an ultimatum which would involve them in a calamitous war. Neither side accepted Saleh's simple statement that I was an inoffensive traveller longing to see one of the most beautiful countries of the world.

We went straight to the Governor's house. The Governor was seated by the window, making the most of the light sea breeze which fanned his room on this hot morning. He was a tall, broad-shouldered man, very dignified in bearing and a typical Yemen aristocrat.

THE LAND OF SHEBA

He welcomed me with many a "How are you?—Quite well?—Thank God". Coffee was served and once again he repeated the kindly formula "How are we? Quite well? Quite comfortable?" I studied my host and fancied I saw a humorous twinkle in his brown eyes.

"Yes, Amil," I answered. "I am comfortable enough now, thank you, but half an hour ago I was the most miserable man in all Yemen." The Amil looked surprised at my unconventional answer, so I explained how I had sat in the fishing-boat grilling like a mackerel, and all through my own folly in forgetting to bring a parasol. After that he dropped formal conversation and we chatted easily. He asked me about the relations between the two Governments, but I answered that this was not my business and that I wished they could settle their little differences so that poor travellers might get on with their business.

"There was once a sherriff who dreamed he had lost his teeth," said the Amil, "so he sent for his Wazir, who, having been told of the dream, declared that the meaning was perfectly clear. 'You will find old age rapidly advancing,' interpreted the Wazir, 'lose all your teeth, and die.' Naturally the sherriff was very angry, imprisoned his Wazir and sent for another adviser. 'Ah,' said the courtier, 'what a favourable dream! You will live to a ripe old age for you will not die until all your teeth have disappeared. We ordinary mortals have no such comforting assurance.'" The story meant, of course, that there are at least two ways of saying the same thing. The Amil meant to suggest that this political quarrel was merely a matter of words. I agreed whole-heartedly, mutual confidence was established, and a little later he promised to forward my request to visit Sanaa.

That evening the Amil informed me by messenger that the Imam had sent his personal invitation to me to visit Sanaa, and had given instructions that the best motor-car—which proved to be a Ford lorry—should be placed at my disposal for the first part of the journey. The Amil very kindly lent me his own mule for the interior journey up to the highlands. I engaged a mule caravan for baggage, and the driver promised to turn up together with his mules at sunrise. Dining that night on the house-top, under a clear sky, with the stars like balls of fire, everything seemed at peace.

A bugle rang out from the neighbouring barracks, and was answered from an outpost two miles distant.

"Quite like old times," I sighed as I lit my cigarette.

It was, for a shot rang out, followed by an answering shot and then a fusillade. The air hummed with flying bullets and I sought shelter behind a wall where a couple of cats calmly joined me. As a matter of fact these cats were the source of all the trouble. A neighbour annoyed by their wailing, had taken a pot shot at them, and his bullet had whizzed past a sheikh's ear. The startled gentleman had promptly replied and then a

THE LAND OF SHEBA

bunya in the bazaar had cried that the bedou were raiding, and the fun commenced, to continue merrily for a lively half-hour.

Next morning Jomary, the caravan leader, appeared protesting loudly. A pilgrim boat had arrived from Jeddah and the pilgrims had commandeered our mules, which meant several days' delay. With invincible optimism, however, Saleh used to warn me each evening to be ready packed and dressed by sunrise.

Finally we managed to recover the mules and, on the morning of our start, they were assembled at dawn, but the drivers talked such a lot that I had plenty of time to pack leisurely before they were ready to load up.

Then a few packs were kicked off amidst blood-curdling oaths from the mule drivers, and it was about 11 a.m. before Saleh and I wished them godspeed, telling them we would follow up and overtake them with the car a little later. They speeded round the corner as far as the next coffee-shop and there they decided it was too hot to continue so they rested till the sun was low.

The Ford lorry, converted with packing-cases into a sort of omnibus, was fairly comfortable until I suddenly found a nail belonging to the packing-cases, and had to comfort myself with a cushion for the rest of the journey. We rocketed gaily over the desert, sometimes finding a camel track, and often a sand dune, and our radiator boiled merrily every hour. We passed small groups of beehive huts, the typical villages

TREASURE OF OPHIR

of the Tihima, and there we would stop to have a cup of coffee whilst our radiator cooled down.

There was little bird life, beyond a landrail or two, a few desert lark (*Prynnhia Gracilis*), two sand grouse, one brain-fever bird, a white egret, some palm doves, and one wood pigeon. These were all that we met on our journey through twenty-five miles of desert land. During spring-time the Tihima can show about a hundred different types, but most of them are migrant birds, and they seldom sing while in Arabian lands, though I have heard the nightingale singing at three o'clock in the afternoon.

We put up no gazelle, though there must have been many a few hundred yards off our track. Sometimes when motoring through the desert I have put up a herd of thirty or forty gazelle, which invariably ran close to the car, and then galloped alongside some twenty or thirty feet distant, finally bounding across our front as if twenty miles per hour were merely gentle exercise to them.

Abdulla M'Haboob the Arab chauffeur proved to be a good driver. He avoided great boulders as he careered over the desert, and eased down with precision when we came to small watercourses crossing our track.

When we reached Behair, Salama ("the woman of peace"), welcomed us, but as soon as she caught sight of a European she declared that she had no food in the house. I pointed out to Saleh that this is what every woman says when an unexpected guest turns up, and

THE LAND OF SHEBA

that if he stuck out for a couple of chickens and a dozen eggs Salama would probably turn up trumps. After much persuasion she changed her mind, and even suggested that she should slaughter a sheep in my honour; but I declared that the chickens would take less time to cook, and would please me much better.

A rainstorm came on, and I welcomed it, for it gave me the opportunity to inspect Salama's house, and incidentally I did not forget to praise Salama's new hat and dress. All women of the Beni Qurah wear the same type of hat and dress, the only variation being that sometimes the dress is made of yellow or scarlet material instead of the usual indigo-dyed cotton. It is cut square, with short sleeves and an open neck, heavily embroidered with bead work. The bead work is also carried out on the hem, but there are no fancy patterns in it, since it is placed there merely for utility, because these portions of the dress are subjected to the greatest wear. The Arab is an extraordinarily poor needle-woman.

The hat is almost identical with the countrywoman's hat in Wales. It is woven from the palm-fan leaf, when the leaf is young and tender with spring sap. If the leaf is left until it is older it does not bleach to the same pure white. Since there is no trimming, a little red fibre is woven into the crown of the hat to give relief to its austerity. Although poor with her needle, the Arab woman is very clever at weaving palm fibre into hats, mats and baskets, and I have often admired this work, which makes the fingers very sore.

TREASURE OF OPHIR

I frankly admired the intricacies of Salama's hat, and my praises gave her a great deal of pleasure. Her hut was spotlessly clean, and well daubed with mud which was stiffened with chopped straw. All round the hut the mud daub was formed into a shelf, about four feet high, on which was kept Salama's tiny stock of household crockery.

When the storm passed we ventured outside again, and found Salama still bending over her charcoal fire, while her daughter Amina ran to and fro on endless messages, gleaning salt, pepper, chillies, sugar and spices. The worst of a coffee-house meal is that it takes so long to prepare, though, when it is prepared, it is usually an excellent one, and by no means marred by the truth of the proverb, "Hunger is the best sauce".

Salama gave us an omelet nicely seasoned, then some excellent soup flavoured with fresh spices. This was followed by stewed chicken flavoured with fresh green chillies, and some fresh baked bread and melted butter.

After the meal Amina brought Saleh's pipe, and prepared it with great care. First she filled the water-bowl to that exact level when it bubbles cheerfully, cools the tobacco to perfection, and yet is not too hard to draw. Then she took two ounces of native raw leaf tobacco, shredded off all the stalk, and wetted the tobacco thoroughly. Over this she piled a heap of glowing charcoal, and we were rewarded by a smoke which is cooler and more fragrant than the choicest cigar. There is some skill and a considerable amount of trouble taken

THE LAND OF SHEBA

in filling and preparing an Arab pipe properly, but when once it is lighted you are well repaid, for the pipe lasts a couple of hours, and serves a group of people. You do not suck the stem, but merely put it to your lips and draw from it.

While we sat over our pipe, Saleh told me the local story of Behair. Two friends took a wager as to which would eat the hottest chillies. The wily Zeki won by strategy, for while his friend munched stolidly till the tears ran down his cheeks, Zeki started a long-winded yarn. "There was an old man of Beha-i-r," said Zeki, expelling his breath, and dwelling lovingly over the cooling syllable. "His business gave him much c-a-r-e," and with the terminal word he again exhaled and cooled his parched tongue. "He was tempted to curse and to swear-r-r. Hullo, Hamoud, what *is* the matter? Surely you don't find these chillies too hot yet?" His tale might have been pointless, but his ruse worked sufficiently well to gain him the wager.

I was searching my memory for a story to cap Saleh's, when our luggage caravan arrived. We admired the way in which Salama and Amina served the men swiftly, quietly, and without any fuss. Half an hour later the pipe was bubbling drowsily, while one by one we dropped off to sleep.

The camp was awake by dawn, and before the sun had climbed the foothills the caravan was on the road. Our car coughed uneasily, but we got started eventually, and covered another fifty miles before we came to a wadi

TREASURE OF OPHIR

(river bed), which ended the motor road. From there we walked on to Obal, a market town that figures large on the map, though it is only a small place, with one very poor coffee-house. These coffee-houses are the inns of the land and can usually serve you with a light meal of fresh milk, new-baked bread and eggs. The Obal coffee-shop was so dirty that we contented ourselves with a cup of fresh milk, and then continued our journey to Hujeila, on mule-back.

Yellow-breasted landrails and orange-coloured weaver birds crossed our path, and the road was busy with country folk, for it was market day at Obal, and they were bringing in their sheep and oxen for sale. The track had a very gradual ascent, and we were coming to the fertile lands at the base of the Yemen foothills. I noted many a farmer with his yoke of oxen and ploughs of the same pattern as those in use in the days of Bilkis and Suleiman. These light ploughs do little more than scratch the soil, but as it is very light, and without loam, it requires no more than a disturbance of the surface to render it fully fertile.

Saleh pressed on, for he had friends at Hujeila, but I took the journey in leisurely fashion, and was well content to keep with the caravan. By and by Mahomedt and Abdulla, two soldiers who were part of the guard which the Amil had furnished from Hodeida, called a halt under one of the banyan trees. They complained that carrying a rifle in the hot Tihima lands was no job for a gentleman. Houdi, one of the mule drivers,

THE LAND OF SHEBA

added his complaint, to the effect that his mule was being worked to death.

As I did not trouble to answer the remarks, they thought they had a sympathetic audience, so all three men commenced a long list of complaints against Jomari, the caravan leader. I let them have their say, and then remarked that at the end of the journey Jomari would have the *backsheesh* to distribute, so perhaps they had better not let him hear of the complaints. The remark acted like a magic charm, and for the next few miles Abdulla, Mahomedt and Houdi were loud in their praise of Jomari, the prince of caravan leaders.

An hour later we reached Hujeila, and found Saleh with plenty of news. The Sheikh of the Beni Qurah had ridden in to give me welcome, and he would call as soon as I was settled down. The telegraph clerk, who was the leading man of the village, bade us make ourselves comfortable at his house. Further, he advised us to stop the night at Hujeila, as the storm was gathering, and, moreover, the Sheikh of the Beni Qurah had ordered a sheep to be slaughtered in my honour.

When Sheikh Abu Hadi called we had a great lunch of omelets, chicken broth, roast lamb, and fresh-picked bananas, and then Sheikh Abu Hadi produced his *pièce de résistance*. He had sent into Obal market for bundles of fresh khat, which is a kind of sorrel. The Yemini will pay almost any price for a bundle of these fresh, tender leaves, which he chews for hours, and the slightly caffein qualities of the khat leaf

TREASURE OF OPHIR

give him exhilaration. I doubt whether the European would gain any effect beyond a severe stomach ache, which is the certain penalty of an overdose of khat. I excused myself, while all the rest of the party settled down to khat chewing, and I had a very comfortable sleep. About 4 p.m. the storm broke, the roof leaked, and we perched wherever we could find a dry spot.

A friend at Aden had given me a mule load of "Scissor" cigarettes, which are excellent light smokes in Arabian climates. The Arabs call them Abu M'gass, and prefer them to any other brand which has yet reached the hinterland. I breached a case of five thousand, and distributed the treasure to all and sundry, knowing full well that my friend's gift would penetrate to many a district where the European has never yet been seen.

CHAPTER IX

THE LAND OF SHEBA—*continued*

NEXT morning we were astir long before sunrise, for a hard day's journey lay in front of us, and we were anxious to get into the shade of the Wadi Hejjam before the sun rose. We had about ten miles to travel up this Wadi, and its stone bed grew more rough as we progressed, but at length we reached the mountain path that took us from the Wadi Hejjam and up some one thousand feet to Wasil.

All the way from Hujeila to Wasil Saleh was feeling sad. At Hodeida he had bought a donkey for five pounds, but unfortunately its lineage and its various recommendations were greater than its performances. There were several prominent points about it, for the poor beast was starved, but it had not sufficient strength for the journey, so Saleh had to leave it at Hujeila, to be sent on later. No man likes to feel he has been made a fool of when buying a mount, and Saleh's feelings had been damaged more than his purse. His spirits rose, however, as we climbed the steep path to Wasil, for we were now coming to the beautiful coffee country, of which this village is an outpost.

TREASURE OF OPHIR

The coffee-house at Wasil was crowded, but we managed to find room for our party, and settled down to drink kishr and idle away the afternoon. Saleh wanted to push on to the next stage, but Jomari said he feared another storm was coming. Jomari of course simply did not want his mules to go any further and his prophecy was a bad one, for the sky at Wasil remained cloudless.

Late in the afternoon our hostess announced that she had cleared a room for me. It had been used for stabling cows, but was now well swept and clean. My sojourn at the inn that night brought home to me very vividly certan phases of New Testament history. In the little room there was the stone manger, where cattle had been feeding so recently, while outside the stars burned bright, and every building was overcrowded with travellers who had not changed appreciably in manners, speech, or dress since that phase of history two thousand years ago.

When the sky paled our caravan woke to activity, and, as the light grew stronger, a scene of beauty unrolled at our feet. Terraced gardens of coffee and green millet spread downward to the morning mist, which still clothed the lowlands. All the horizon, as far as the eye could travel, was girt with mountains of these terraced gardens, changing to every hue as the rising sun swept away the darkness and the mists of dawn. We were travelling on the military road which the Turks had built, and, viewing these rich lands, I felt sorry that

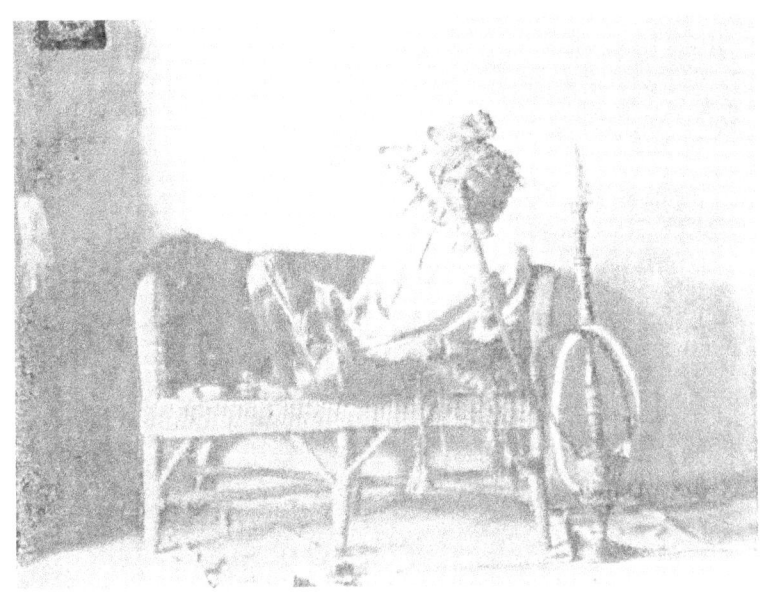

An Arab With His Pipe

Members of the Caravan

[Facing page 132

THE LAND OF SHEBA

they have been for so long under the rule of a military people against whom there is that terrible saying: "Where the Turk treads grass does not grow".

These garden lands of Yemen could provide sufficient food for all the desert wastes of Arabia, if only the transport were sufficiently developed for the foodstuffs to be got away under economical conditions. In ancient times the Arabs developed camel transport, while the trade winds gave to sea transport a northern flow for merchandise for six months, and a return southern flow for the remaining six months of a year. Under those conditions inland transport kept pace with sea transport, and was efficient, and all that could be desired. Now that sea transport is independent of the trade winds it has outpaced camel transport, and as the land transport methods have not been brought up-to-date, Arabia is a poverty-stricken land. I might interpolate here that the present Imam of Yemen fully realizes this point, and after discussing transport and other problems with us, His Highness has given orders for road surveys to be undertaken throughout Yemen. His lands will probably have better roads and better trade outlets in the near future, and El Bustani, the garden lands of Yemen, will benefit accordingly.

Our road was a broken one, but good enough for mule transport from Wasil onwards. We climbed three thousand feet in four hours, and then descended a few hundred feet to reach the town and fortress of Menakha, a place to which the Turks sent some

TREASURE OF OPHIR

British prisoners during the Great War. Those prisoners furnished the Government House with desks and panelling, and if by any chance these pages should meet the eye of any of those men, they may like to know that their work still stands in perfect condition and is greatly admired by the townspeople.

Anywhere in the highlands of Yemen you can get excellent almonds and raisins, which are produced mainly from Sanaa districts. They are splendid food for the traveller, and take the place of the piece of chocolate carried by the European. Saleh had also brought with him some Arab biscuits, which are rather dry and powdery, not very appetizing, in fact; but the traveller soon learns the truth of the maxim, "Hunger is the best sauce", and we found the biscuits very enjoyable when we stopped and had a light breakfast at the coffee-house we found in the Wadi Mefhak.

In the Wadi we put up five chikor, and fine healthy birds they were. The Arabian chikor is a red-legged partridge, with a black cap, slate-blue body, and black stripes to his ribs. He is very different to the Indian chikor, but, like his Indian cousin, he tames easily. Indian troops, while at Aden, would buy the birds readily, and used them as game cocks.

Years later, at Aden, I bought some of the birds, as they are excellent for the table. While they were being fattened, their soft call of "Boy Boyee" charmed my wife, and saved their lives. One, in particular, became a great pet, and we called him "Cheeky". He would

THE LAND OF SHEBA

follow my wife up and down the stairs uttering his soft call, and when our servant brought the morning cup of tea, "Cheeky" would come hopping into the room, and would jump on the bed. If my wife pretended to be asleep, he would peck her hair to waken her, and even learned to open her eyes by lifting an eyelid with his beak, though this was a trick which made me rather nervous. He would never help himself to toast or biscuit, but waited until a morsel was broken for him.

In Wadi Mefhak insect and bird life were plentiful. We saw a good many landrails of different types, and, though we did not see any Birds of Paradise, we were told they are plentiful. One of the nicest birds of Yemen is the *asfari*, a red-breasted linnet, that sings divinely and cages well; it is, however, rather delicate, and all efforts to import it to Constantinople have proved failures. In the Wadi we saw plenty of *asfari*, and several other bird types. We met plenty of butterflies, including fritillaries, orange-tips, scarlet-tips, and sulphur-yellows. We saw a dead snake, which was about four feet long, of thick girth, with slate grey back and a light belly. I did not manage to identify it, but think it was some form of rat snake and not very poisonous. My old mule walked quietly along, and took no notice of it; but Abdulla, who was walking beside me, trying to cajole a dollar from me with which to buy khat, tripped over it, and got the start of his life.

TREASURE OF OPHIR

Now and then we met little chameleons, deliciously ugly little fellows, who are normally of a blue tint, but change their hues slightly to match the rocks on which they bask. When we approached they would bob their heads and look very fierce, till they realized they had met visitors whom they could not scare away. Then, with a whisk of the tail, they would vanish behind the nearest boulder.

As we neared Suk el Khamis (the Thursday market town) I was amused to note a ploughman carrying his plough over his shoulder. The native plough is only a log of wood, with a wooden stake set roughly at right-angles to it. The plough seldom weighs more than twenty pounds, but is sufficiently heavy for the light volcanic soil of Yemen.

All the hill-sides were terraced with hanging gardens, and these terraces represent generations of patient labour. They are formed by walls of the stones gathered when clearing the soil, and there are many uncultivated mountain-sides which seem mere desert land, but which would respond to the same rich culture of hanging gardens, if there were a proper demand for the fruits of Yemen. When I returned to Aden, after many months in Yemen, I was met with "superior intelligence", and told that my enthusiasm colours impracticable dreams. I find that the past travellers of that happy land were faced with the same polite scepticism. When a few ounces of good "grey matter" are imported to these ancient lands of Sabbea, we shall

THE LAND OF SHEBA

soon enjoy the exports of a land that is larger than India, though less known than the Polar Regions.

The coffee-house keepers at Suq el Khamis were delighted to welcome the European visitor, and suggested that we should take the nearest available rooms. Saleh protested that they were very dirty, and we turned a deaf ear to the assertions that no travellers of the last fortnight had made any complaints. Eventually Beda bestirred herself and swept out two rooms for us, and having once roused herself to action, she was hospitality herself. She suggested that we might like some bananas, mangoes, apricots and pears, for the fruit season of Sanaa was just commencing, and we were now in the lands where we could get a foretaste of it. The season was rather early, so most of the fruit was unripe, but it was very welcome whilst we were waiting for the main meal, which had to be cooked over charcoal fires.

Once Saleh had got his pipe going he told of a great surprise he had in store for me. He had telegraphed to friends at Sanaa, and they would have a car to meet us at Boaam, our next stopping-place, which we should reach after a few hours' ride the next morning. Former experience had taught me that an Arab motor journey was a thing to be avoided if possible, so I was not overjoyed, though I was not churl enough to tell Saleh so.

Following our usual custom, we started next morning before sunrise and reached Boaam before 9 a.m. It was market day, and the little town was full of life. There is a mountain stream skirting Boaam, so we sat

TREASURE OF OPHIR

under the bridge with a large dish of fruit, while we waited for the car to turn up. Time passed pleasantly enough. We demolished all the fruit, and had a refreshing wash in the cold waters of the stream, but we saw no signs of the car, which was by now long overdue.

Saleh said he feared the car was not coming, but I thought the suggestion was too good to be true. However, as nothing appeared, we mounted our mules and took the road. As we climbed the hills, Saleh gave a whoop of joy, and an ancient Ford car rattled up to us. We were welcomed by Saleh's friends, and though the car was already well loaded, we squeezed into it somehow. The friend who was driving was an officer of the Imam's Air Force, and, although he did not pretend to be a great aviator, he was ready enough to live up to the reputation for speed gained by the officers of the world's aviation services.

There was many a sharp hairpin bend on that mountain road and when my heart was not in my mouth it was in my boots, anticipating the next swerve. With rather a sharp descent the mountain road wound down to the plains, and we then had fifteen miles of level going before us. The road looked reasonably good, and we settled down to comfortable anticipations of a lunch at Sanaa. Our friends explained how dreary we should have found this last stage if we had been on mule back, and we replied with every compliment that a good imagination could furnish.

THE LAND OF SHEBA

Suddenly there was a splutter, and the engine stopped. Our driver threw up his hands in despair, for the petrol had run out, we had not got a spare tin, and the nearest supply was at Sanaa. We were some miles from Boaam, so we could not telegraph our plight to Sanaa, but after about one hour's wait we managed to borrow a donkey, and one of the party galloped off to Sanaa and fetched us a fresh supply of petrol. We replenished, and raced madly for the city, for the gates are shut at sunset. We anxiously watched the shadows growing longer, and just as the sun was sinking behind the hills, we won by a narrow margin.

I had asked permission to visit Sanaa at a time when I had no reason to expect a favourable answer, but we were treated with kindness from the moment we arrived on Yemen shores. On arrival at Sanaa we were shown to a charming house, and told to use it as our own and to ask for all that we required, because we were the guests of His Highness the Iman. For three days we were given the fullest hospitality, and no one came to call while we settled into our new home. This period of three days is in accord with Arab custom, but a European visitor had no reason to expect Arab privileges to be extended to him.

After these three days His Highness sent word that he would be pleased to see me in audience the next morning. The Imam's Palace is a large building situated in the north-west corner of Sanaa city. It is

TREASURE OF OPHIR

Turkish built, and not very artistic in design, but His Highness is planning to erect a new palace that shall be built as a replica of an ancient palace of three thousand years ago, and which will be reconstructed from building materials of the older palace ruins. I hope that he will carry out these designs, and so build one of the most interesting dwellings in the world. The present palace is a large building facing east, with a northern wing containing the audience-chambers, the whole structure being surrounded by a thick wall some nine feet high.

From our house in Bir Azal I rode to the west gate of Sanaa City, and after skirting the palace wall for a hundred yards, I entered the Imam's Palace. A flight of steps gave entrance to the north wing and here I was welcomed by one of the house officers, who had been busy superintending the hospitalities of the past two days. He took me by the hand and asked me to remove my shoes. An Arab will enter his house wearing his turban, but would not dream of taking his soiled shoes into living quarters. The officer apologized for a custom which he supposed was new to me, but I replied with the tale of the Indian, who reported that the English were a topsy-turvy race, who readily discarded their clean hats, but wear their muddy boots when entering rooms. I assured him that I had no desire to show such contrariness.

We entered the audience-room, which was furnished in Arab style, with many carpets and cushions,

THE SOUTHERN GATE, SANAA

[Facing page 140

THE LAND OF SHEBA

but no tables or chairs. Seated on one of the cushion piles, a middle-aged man was reading some Arab papers, while his grandchild, a small girl of four, played by his side. He looked up, and I made my salaams to my host, His Highness Imam Yehia bin Imam Hahmud Hameed ed Deen, the King of Yemen.

He is a well-built man of middle height. His well-developed forehead, his keen eyes, and soft, yet firm speech, showed him to be a ruler who is well fitted to control the fairest lands of a restless peninsula. Over coffee, the Imam welcomed me to his country with many a kind and courtly phrase, and as soon as the opportunity presented itself I thanked His Highness for his many kindnesses and hospitalities.

I suggested that I should now find my own lodgings, and shift for myself, but the Imam laughed away such suggestions, and assured me that, whether I stayed for a week or for a year, he desired that I should consider myself his guest. His invitation was by no means an empty formality, for I stayed at Sanaa three months, and was his guest for all that time. Of course I took care to spend my full household expenses in other ways than by purchasing the necessities of life. At the end of this period we returned to Aden, and His Highness sent us down by the road which Queen Bilkis journeyed three thousand years ago, when she travelled to Palestine. For that journey His Highness provided both escort and caravan, while he sent mes-

TREASURE OF OPHIR

sages to various Governors *en route,* who entertained me on our arrival at their towns.

. . . . .

Later, much later, I asked permission to return to Sanaa, and once more enjoyed the same hospitality, with kindness and welcome from the Governors of each province through which we passed.

Soon after my arrival on the occasion of my first visit His Highness had a kindly thought, which was of the greatest value to me. He sent the Court Historian to give me any information on the subject of my search, which involves some rather abstruse details of Arab history. Then some two months after my arrival, an old friend of mine, the Foreign Minister to the Imam, returned from a tour in Italy. During many a pleasant afternoon spent with my old friend, I learned something of the life of Yemen, and of customs which have remained unchanged for thousands of years.

These customs I hope to explain whilst submitting my proofs of the location of Ophir.

PART TWO

CHAPTER I

THE TRUTH OF GENESIS

In Genesis we may trace the Ophir tribe from its origin, which is also the origin of Middle Eastern man, and so onward until we find the tribe founding its famous seaport. This tribe had built ships and developed harbours; the call of the sea took its people to other lands, and their ventures brought them wealth. With growing power they ultimately became the leaders of other tribes. The Middle East had awakened to its glorious era, a time some three thousand years ago, when Arabia really enjoyed a Golden Age.

Among their seven kingdoms, the gold-bearing lands and countries of precious stones achieved world fame, and they traded happily with the Far East. They were one great family in a country larger than France, a Semitic family that had its family quarrels, fierce and sudden, though they were spared those racial wars which have ruined other lands.

They were immune from invasion or from peaceful penetration, for their geographical situation gave them full security. To north and west their lands were encircled and isolated by great mountain ranges; to south and east they were sea-girt, and their coasts seemed iron-bound and were fringed with desert wastes, so uninviting that no traveller could guess the riches which lay further inland.

Their sea coasts were not really iron-bound, for those rocky coasts and steep cliffs held many clefts and hidden harbours which were unapproachable for the foreigner, although they gave to the native the best of harbour shelter. The desert shores were mainly coral fringed and the dangers of coral navigation were added to the uninviting appearance of waste lands. So the natives lived within an ideal land, the dream land of philosophers. Theirs was "an island within an island" —Sheba, the Jezirat within Jezirat ul Arab—the Island of Arabia.

The first historical evidence of the Ophir Land appears in the early chapters of Genesis, where Havilah, Jobab and Ophir are mentioned as sons of Joktan. This is evidently a tribal allusion, with geographical location to it. But tracing back to earlier Genesis history we note that the historians evidently had no intention of allowing the locality of the Garden of Eden to be lost to history. They give us Euphrates and Hiddekel, rivers which are easy to identify as the modern Euphrates and Tigris; and then they tell us a good deal about the land of Havilah, for we learn "the River Pison encompasseth the whole land of Havilah, where there is gold, And the gold of that land is good, and there is onyx stone and bdellium." At first sight it would seem that,

ON THE BANKS OF THE EUPHRATES

[*Facing page* 146

THE TRUTH OF GENESIS

though the Pison is lost, we should have no difficulty in finding Havilah by mineral location.

However, gold is one of the most widely distributed of metals, and the Biblical onyx stone is not necessarily the onyx stone of to-day. Bdellium is at present an unknown substance, so we must first try to find the lost river Pison, and corroborate our evidence by mineral location of Havilah, to assist us in arriving at the location of Ophir.

Travelling to and fro in the Persian Gulf, I was able to note its shores and its depths. These depths are not ocean soundings, and they clearly represent a basin valley that has been flooded.

Mountain ranges practically encircle the Persian Gulf and its littoral. The eastern extremity is the entrance called the Straits of Ormuz, and eastward of these straits the soundings run to true ocean depths. Not only have we got the strong suggestion that the Persian Gulf is a submerged basin valley, but also we have direct evidence that the southern shores of this valley were water-bearing.

Indeed, without further deduction, we can almost make the direct statement that the waters of the Persian Gulf have submerged one or more rivers. The pearl-fishers of Bahrein are very strong in their assertions that their pearls owe their unique quality and colour to the presence of fresh-water seepage from the floor of the Persian Gulf; indeed, the fact is so well established that in the Farisan pearl banks the merchants will increase their credit advances when there is a heavy rainy season. Not only is there the great fresh-water spring that wells upward in Bahrein harbour, but the banks, with their lustrous pearls, stretch far east of Bahrein, and all along the Hasa coast, which is a water-bearing land, with many a bottomless pit of water in it.

I am going to suggest that the lost river junction of Eden is located in a basin valley which was inundated by the Great Flood, and is now hidden by the waters of the Persian Gulf.

The bulk of the evidence for this theory lies in Genesis, and instead of following the lead of many pseudo-scientists, and condemning that evidence unheard, we shall need to examine its leading points from the commencement of human history.

Orthodox theologians with their somewhat limited outlook, and self-styled "higher critics", have played havoc with Genesis evidence, until now most of the old tales would seem very good to tell to children, but not very much use for intelligent historical analysis.

The "higher critics" have asserted that Genesis is a collection of extracts from mythological histories, which are mostly of Sumerian and Babylonian origin. Yet they assert that this collection of mythological stories is interwoven so as to give a consistent theme of monotheism. Can one conceive anything quite so illogical? How could a collection of mere myths combine to form a history which is immortal, and which has withstood the criticisms of all ages and of countless

THE TRUTH OF GENESIS

creeds? Can one suppose that three great religions, Judaism, Christianity and Islam are all based merely on the insecure foundations of mythology?

Genesis is the oldest history in the world, or rather a collection of ancient histories, records, and traditions, which are by no means mythical, and the Babylonian legends are merely the outpost echoes of that seat of learning of which Eden was the western boundary. By an intelligent examination of Genesis we shall find that the orthodox theologian is perfectly right, within his narrow limits, which are entirely self-imposed. But, alas, we shall find that the "higher critic", with his lack of knowledge, has consistently put the cart before the horse.

The old history is unnamed, but commences with the word Beresith which means "In the beginning".

As its story commences from the beginning of things, and holds a continuous theological theme, the book has been incorporated in the Old Testament under the name of Genesis. Tradition is strong that Genesis was written by Moses, the prophet and leader. "Higher criticism" shows that Genesis cannot have been written by Moses, but by no means proves that it was not compiled and edited by him. Unchanged except for errors of translation and almost uncriticised, it passed through the Dark Ages. Superstition and the power of Orthodoxy prevented intelligent criticism, and also prevented full appreciation of this most interesting history.

TREASURE OF OPHIR

Early in the nineteenth century A.D. Charles Darwin commenced to show that scientific evidence was contrary to the orthodox interpretations of Genesis.

In England, at this period, the Church controlled all intelligent criticism of the Holy Bible, but unfortunately the Church did not fully realize that there are possibly interpretations which differ from the accepted orthodox interpretation, while they in no way alter the truths which Orthodoxy has developed. The hindrance of Orthodoxy has proved beneficial on the whole. "A little learning is a dangerous thing", and only "a little learning" was available to the unorthodox of the nineteenth century.

That little learning produced an agnosticism and a materialistic outlook pitiable to the present generation. Until the commencement of the twentieth century theologians stoutly upheld the truths of Genesis, though they did not develop those truths with the light of scientific knowledge which was commencing to dawn on Western society.

Orthodoxy has discouraged independent thought, which is necessary to the proper investigation of Biblical problems. The consequences were inevitable, and they seem to have been hastened by the Great War which overwhelmed Western lands, for men who had faced life in its crudest aspects were no longer content to accept the platitudes of an orthodox teaching which does not seem to support the truth.

Orthodoxy was weakened and Biblical truths were

THE TRUTH OF GENESIS

assailed with criticisms that have frequently been hostile. The hostility may be regrettable, yet it has awakened an interest in Biblical matters which was dormant in past decades. Meanwhile many leaders of theological thought seem to have abandoned the truth in their panic, but the truth of all Biblical history is likely to be established with rapidity if orthodox theologians are prepared to accept the assistance of unorthodox investigators.

In the following pages I attempt to show that the oldest history in the world holds many truths that are at present being abandoned, though those truths have not as yet received full or proper investigation. When you regard it as a scientific record and trace each piece of evidence in its historic order, then Genesis becomes very convincing. I propose to go into the Flood history with some care, since that phase especially has so often been condemned by persons who are not qualified to express opinions on a subject of which they are, in fact, totally ignorant.

But we must start at the beginning if we wish to appreciate the whole romance of the Middle East.

CHAPTER II

IN THE BEGINNING

THE earlier ages were not suitable for human existence, for there seems to have been no fresh water and no minerals until after the waters deposited their mineral salts during the "seventh day", the geological rest-period. When the waters were freed from their minerals they were capable of evaporation on a scale that was not possible at an earlier stage.

This deposition of minerals and evaporation caused a definite change in atmospheric conditions, and most of the giant animals died off: they have left fossils on land and some representatives among the giant terrestrial mammals. In the sea we have a very large number of representatives of the early ages. Whales, giant octopi and sea-snakes of over one hundred feet in length are a few of the obvious representatives of a world which would be entirely prehistoric were it not for the evidence of Genesis.

Before Man walked this earth as a physical being, atmospheric changes had caused a marked variation in vegetation and the "herb of the field" came to replace

IN THE BEGINNING

the giant ferns of earlier ages. The world was then fit for human habitation and Man appeared.

In all probability humanity evolved in every locality that was fit for human habitation, but Genesis is not concerned with vague generalities. It deals mainly with the people who were the direct ancestors of the Semitic races and gives but slight mention to persons and events which are not directly concerned with Semitic history.

As far as Genesis history is concerned, man originated in the desert somewhere West of Eden. This seems to place the commencement of Adamite races in the locality of the heights of Ararat, probably in much the same place as the one in which they recommenced their development after the Ark grounded and rested. After indicating a place of origin, the history traces evolution through gradual stages; from the unisexual, who apparently had no speech, to the Adam race, who had developed intelligence almost to the human stage, when they became bisexual and what we understand as humans.

So far as the Middle East is concerned, Man apparently came into being some two geological ages after the appearance of vertebrate animal-life. Genesis tells us this, and biology gives a general support to the same suggestion. We are informed that "Man (Hebrew, *Ish*) was formed from the dust of the ground". Here we must note that the orthodox theologian of the old school seems to have unnecessarily insisted on reading the singular for what is really the generic term. "Ish was formed . . ." The word Ish (or Man) obviously refers to a type rather than to one isolated human being. The latter supposition would be dead against the laws or practices of Nature.

Furthermore, that suggestion does not seem in accordance with the literature of an Eastern language, where the generic (or tribal) plural is constantly employed. But the statement that Man in general was formed from the dust of the ground and started as a unisexual seems entirely in accord with scientific evidence. We still have the unisexual as a common form of animal life, of which the algæ of the pools and ditches are an example.

In view of this we can accept the rather surprising evidence of Genesis and realize that Ish was a mere unisexual animal, in some respects no higher than the most primitive worm. Yet there is another point for consideration, and regarding this the English translation is somewhat obscure. Ish was apparently endowed with the breath of life from a source higher than that awarded to other brute creation, and we may perhaps suggest that this faculty gave to him the well-developed reasoning-power which is scarcely developed in other animals.

Ish probably arrived about 500,000 B.C.—possibly a great deal earlier and probably no later than that date. A late arrival in animal life, he was well favoured in the accident of birth. In the lone heights of steppe lands some 7,000 feet above sea-level, Ish was almost free from the depredations of carnivoræ. In his initial

IN THE BEGINNING

stages he was able to develop intelligence free from the handicaps of fear, and with that start he was more favoured than the other animals. In all probability he started life as an ugly and helpless sort of mammal, something akin to the ape. In the initial stages he was in many ways inferior to other animals, for he had not yet gained that age-long experience which is inaccurately classified as instinct. Moreover, he had not yet gained sexual knowledge and all the wisdom which that knowledge imparts.

Try to picture the first man that ever was, lying alone in the heights of Ararat. Feelings of thirst and hunger caused him to stir. Directly his eyes were opened he faced the light, as every animal born above ground will do. He could satisfy his first thirst with the dew, but hunger forced him to action as he grubbed for food. Later, thirst and curiosity took him to the mountain streams. Here he found food was more plentiful. Vegetation, roots, grubs, worms and mud-eels all came alike to the maw of Ish the Primitive.

As the early hours of the day are the most vigorous, Ish, in his aimless wanderings, unwittingly attracted by light, made a definite and continuous amount of Easting. He commenced life in the highlands; forces of gravity took him downhill, thus he was led to wander towards the Eastern Lowlands.

When his animal needs were satisfied he slept, and, when he awoke, kept near the banks of the stream, because there vegetation and water were easy to obtain.

TREASURE OF OPHIR

His stream met other mountain rivulets, and so he met others of his kind who had obeyed the same natural impulses as he had done. So we figure hundreds of the unisexual Ish working their way downhill and meeting gradually to form that first people with whom Genesis is concerned, the Ish or Man from whom the Adam tribes were descended.

Almost certainly Ish was dumb, for speech is imitative, and in his original home he had little example and no incentive to exert his imitative faculties. Can you picture the scene when Ish the lonesome met another of his type? It gives us a hint how language first was formed. The Primitive bared his fangs in a fierce grin and remained motionless, petrified with fear. At length the pent-up breath came purling through his teeth, "Sss-s-sh!"—and so Ish was his name.

Feeding and grubbing for roots was a common instinct, so Ish became gregarious, eating his way through the lowlands. In those lowlands he encountered a decisive factor, which has not yet been recognized by the biologists. This point is well worth noticing, for it gives us the clue to the story of Adam and Eve and the Forbidden Fruit.

Primitive peoples eat to live, and what is plentiful becomes their only diet. I have spent a long time amongst somewhat primitive races, and the monotony of their diet becomes appalling to one of more cultivated tastes. On one occasion I met an Arab who had reverted to the simple life in its most primitive form. He was

IN THE BEGINNING

living at Ras Mouni, an uninviting headland off Socotra Island. He had several wives, and he threw stones at them when they were so inquisitive as to approach his visitor. He had no cooking-pots, no grain growing near his cave, and indeed, no visible means of subsistence.

"What do you eat? Where do you drink?" I asked.

He knocked some shell-fish off the rocks and scooped some water from the sands of the seashore. He said nothing, for action was his answer. His mode of life gave me an insight into the existence of Ish, who worked his way down the River Euphrates to its junction with the River Pison that we are searching for. If I passed any of his early history without comment, then destructive criticism would suggest my investigations are based on unreliable foundations.

In the Euphrates Valley Ish came across the date-tree. The date-tree is easy to climb and the harvest is easy to gather. Ish had found a food that was very palatable, very sustaining, and far more accessible than the majority of the fruits. During the date season, which is in the summer and autumn months, dates became his staple diet. Unfortunately, however, this fruit is not at all suitable as a staple diet, for the ripened date is very rich in sugar and consequently overheating to the blood, so that a prolonged diet of dates promotes excessive sexual urge. Ish the unisexual had no outlet for his repressed sexual instincts, though meanwhile a date diet was awakening those instincts to unnatural activity.

TREASURE OF OPHIR

Suppressed sexual instincts usually lead to violent action, such as we now classify as criminal instinct. Picture Ish the Primitive, his blood overheated and his brain aflame with murderous thoughts, creeping behind some unsuspecting mate and smashing in his skull with club or stone. In all probability the summer and autumn (the date season) became a season of violence. The Apple is the Forbidden Fruit of tradition, derived from Greek mythology, but the apple does not give any of the effects described in Genesis, and moreover, the apple is not a fruit of the hot Euphrates Valley.

At length Ish realized that the date could not be eaten with impunity, and a tribal tabu was placed on the tree, not necessarily a verbal tabu, for there is Genesis evidence that at this stage language was very undeveloped. But a silent tabu offers no difficulty, for in the present day the goats and sheep have placed a tabu on Deadly Nightshade, and that tabu is generally obeyed by their species, though it is disobeyed with sufficient frequency to show that it is a tabu and not an instinct.

The date had, however, done its work, and unisexual man longed for his mate. " Iss-ah," he sighed.

. . . . .

Iss had reached the Eastern limit of his parklands—lands which are generally styled The Garden of Eden. This oasis supplied all his simple needs, and he had no incentive to urge him to cross the river junction. Through the countless ages, perhaps over a

IN THE BEGINNING

period of 500,000 years, he had changed in appearance. His ape-like, hairy skin had become a thick hide, suitable for his existence in a park-land of thick undergrowth. He became Ed-Dum or Adam, the Red Man, and the race of Adam was evolved whilst the race of Ish had not yet become extinct.

At this stage the history reads easily if we accept the name Adam as a generic term. Later on it becomes more distinctly tribal, and then, as the history becomes more definite, Adam is employed in the individual sense; to be re-employed again in a generic sense at the point where Genesis furnishes a wonderful tribal genealogy, which I shall attempt to translate into modern language.

The Race of Adam or the Red People had the animal instincts of Ish, but were not handicapped by any hindrances of fear, though all other animal life knew and profited by the instincts of fear for the preservation of their species. The Race of Adam, however, lived in a Garden where there were "beasts of the field", but those lands were almost certainly free from predatory animals of any size. Possibly these cool lands were snake-free, though this sounds rather a contradiction to Bible history.

Freed from the handicaps of fear, Adam was able to develop intelligence. More intelligent than Ish, he studied the animals and probably derived speech from first exercising his vocal chords in imitation of animal-sounds, for Adam was able to name the animals. Also he noted them during their mating seasons and learnt to acquire sexual longing.

"Ish-h," he sighed. "Ish-h, Ish-h-ah," and, at last, Isshah, his mate, came to him, for Isshah was the name of the first woman.

For a long period the Adamite history remains tribal rather than individual. Later it refers to the Sheikh Adam, who was head of the Adam tribe. We are told that Adam called his mate Isshah, and then after that statement we find the first tribal law. It was to some extent a matriarchal law, for it commanded that a man should be absorbed into the woman's tribe. Consequently none of the prediluvian tribes were of long duration, for the law naturally discouraged mating outside the tribe, where tribal property would go from the man's tribe to the tribe of his wife. That caused a lack of fresh stock, and each prediluvian tribe died out within one thousand years. The Semitic tribes later revised this law, and there are many Semitic families in existence at the present time who can trace their ancestry for several thousand years.

Shortly before the Flood the first tribal law was either annulled or broken generally. The Second Chapter of Genesis closes with a statement that shows the primitive state of the tribe at that stage of their history. Both men and women were naked and unashamed of their nakedness.

CHAPTER III

THE FALL OF MAN?

THE Theologians speak about the Fall of Man, but the Scientists say that human progress shows no evidence of a setback. Genesis, the history of the Adamite race, steers a middle path between these contradictions. It shows us that, from a theological standpoint, Man probably experienced a very definite setback, but from the point of view of biology, Man received an urge which has made him the lord of brute creation.

This phase of the history deals with a sexual problem, but as a frank discussion of such intimate details might not be fitting to a religious history, the discussion is clothed in allegory. The allegorical form is indicated by the opening sentence of that Third Chapter. The whole chapter is a masterpiece of poetic prose, for it does not disguise its truths, furnishes intimate details of unique historical interest, and gives us a great insight into the development of tribal life.

At the same time it gives to the unlearned a beautiful story that develops the theological theme of Genesis. Western theology has adopted that tale to its requirements, and in doing so has made some slight changes that interfere with the historical truths of Genesis. Unfortunately, many of the points of that story are not obvious to Western peoples. For instance, there are only a very few Western people that have had the opportunity to observe that "subtil serpent", the lizard, darting in and out among the date palms.

First let us free ourselves of a few popular misconceptions. In Western lands almost every child is told the story of Adam and Eve and the Apple. To be historically accurate we should note that that story is merely an adaption of Greek mythology to a Middle Eastern history, which, though allegorical, is very precise and accurate. As I have already noted, the apple is not mentioned, because apples never grew, nor could grow, in a land which is free from frost and can never have known much frost within the ages of humanity.

It was Isshah (the Woman), not Eve, who persuaded Man to eat the Forbidden Fruit. Adam is brought in later as a tribal leader, and Eve does not appear in the history until much later still, where her name is introduced as headwoman of the tribe as soon as that office became necessary for the tribal organization of the Red or Adam race.

Whilst Ish and Adam tilled their gardens, making little rivulets and mud channels to irrigate the beds. Isshah gathered her fruits. Her duties took her further afield as the fruits near the homestead were exhausted, and as she wandered through the undergrowth she was scratched with acacia thorn, bitten by ants, and

IN THE BEGINNING

stung by red hornets: everywhere in the river oasis she met the tabu tree, with its golden harvest of fruit drooping temptingly close to her reach.

She would sit down to rest in its shade, and she watched the tree lizard darting among the golden branches. The "subtil serpent" seemed to live on date fruit, though in reality he was catching the flies which were intoxicated with fermented date sap. She knew the "subtil serpent" as her friend, for the house lizard catches the mosquitoes in the mud hut, fights the tarantula spider, and even the scorpion, so it seemed to her that the little-legged serpent gave the answer to the question that was ever present in her mind, namely: Was the fruit really a deadly poison?

That tabu was ages old. It had lasted from the dim ages when there was no Isshah on this world, and the reason for the prohibition was hidden in ancient folk-lore. The lizard seemed to thrive on the fruit, and so she took some, tasted it, and came to no harm. The result was a foregone conclusion. Day after day the women made their experiments, and once again the date was working its mysterious force.

At length woman grew bold in her knowledge. This fruit that was so delicious gave her the knowledge that seems the most important of animal wisdom, for in its own land the date is regarded as a sexual tonic. She gave it to her mate, who accepted it with but little hesitation, for amongst privitive people the woman is in charge of the commissariat, and her word is law.

TREASURE OF OPHIR

Here is a small personal experience to emphasize that point. Once I lived for a time at an Arab fishing village. I had my own hut, and the womenfolk came each morning to sell me the small requirements of bachelor existence.

A man named Hamzeh came to me one evening, and asked me to give him some dinner, explaining that his wife Anisah had told him to be home by sunset, but that as sunset is the time when sea fishing is at its best, he had stayed at work. When he did return Anisah told him that the evening meal was finished, and that he would get nothing that night.

I gave Hamzeh a meal, but in so doing I made a mistake. The next morning I was informed that the hens had failed to lay and that there were no eggs. Also, there were no fish, as the catch had been small, and was required for the nearest market. And the women regretted they could not spare any chickens until the laying season recommenced.

I took a tin of bully beef from my store, but I could not bring myself to open it, for bully beef is unappetizing stuff, so I made a light breakfast off a couple of cigarettes. But hunger sharpens the wits, and I soon made a good guess at the reason for the sudden food shortage. I then sent the tin of bully beef to Anisah with a message to the effect that I was sorry there was a famine on, but that she was welcome to share my poor supplies.

The women evidently concluded that the Englishman

THE FALL OF MAN

had learned his lesson, which was, not to interfere in domestic arrangements, for next morning there was a good breakfast, the hens were laying, the catch of fish was plentiful, and chickens were available.

I have inserted this story to illustrate how, under primitive conditions, each sex has to do a full share of work. Woman collects and cooks the food, and in that department she holds complete control. Woman had apparently proved to her satisfaction that the tabu on the date was ineffective, so she brought that food to her husband and bade him eat.

One supposes that this fruit, so easily obtainable, became the staple diet once again, and the tribe suffered the natural consequences. Amongst wild life the rutting season is definitely in the spring time, but to this primitive people the Call of the Mate came again in the late autumn, which is not the rutting season. I give late autumn as the time, because the date fruit had then been in season some months, and by early autumn was fully ripened and at its greatest power.

The inhabitants of Eden found the call was so strong that they were forced to adopt some form of clothing. They wove fig leaves, probably using string-palm fibre for their twine. Then Sheikh Adam, the leader of the intelligent tribe, gave interpretation to the thoughts that were disturbing them.

The tabu was broken; and when the evening breezes came rippling over the desert and rustling through the leaves of their forest home, it seemed to

TREASURE OF OPHIR

Adam that a vengeful God was walking in His garden. The message Adam received is written in the light of later experience, for as we read the tribal history of the Adamites, we can trace the stages at which they gradually came to the full experience that enabled them to give a complete interpretation to the lesson they commenced to learn in the oasis Garden of Eden.

Woman, with her sexual powers developed beyond those of the wild animal, no longer enjoyed the full recuperative power of the wild. By her own initiative she had started the human race towards Progress, and placed it on the road that it has followed since those dim ages, but she paid the full price. Man found the need for providing his mate with more substantial clothing than the dress of fig leaves, so he hunted for skins, and his hunting took him farther afield than his wooded oasis. He met the wild cat, lynx, lion, wild dog, hyena, and camel. With development of sex and with a strenuous life of hunting, the Adamite developed his manhood.

Old-age instincts reawakened, and he desired the wide horizons of his forefathers. The limits of his garden were too small for him, so once again the tribe went on trek, journeying eastward to the unknown. In uncultivated desert they met thorn, thistle, and the hardships of pioneer life. The mention of the thistle is particularly interesting, for the thistle is not prominent in those latitudes at present, and its presence helps us in our later deductions.

The Wall and South Gate, Sanaa

A Welcome at Seihut
These Arabs are said to be Unfriendly!

[*Facing page* 166

THE FALL OF MAN

In swamp lands they encountered sickness and malaria, and among the burning rocks and dunes they found the legless serpent, the poisonous little sand asp that strikes for the heel. They tried to turn back, but were baffled by the sword of the flaming Arabian sun which turned every way. They were also disheartened by their folklore of which we have some hint.

From a peaceful oasis tribe they had progressed to the fighting stage, in which their God was armed with an invincible flaming sword. Their garden home was lost to them for ever, and they were left with traditions of an earthly paradise, which held the Tree of Life and its cure-all properties that humanity still searches for in the patent medicines of to-day. They formed their folklore to a poetic prose, which they have handed down to immortality.

When the Adamite tribe resumed their bedu status, it was necessary for them to have both a headman and a headwoman. Father Adam, or Sheikh Adam, was the head of the Adamites, and to his wife he gave the title Eve, Mother of All, for she was mother of all the tribe. An Assyrian stone suggests that man first made his appearance in the Middle East some 490,600 B.C., and that suggests this phase of Adamite history may well be as early as you choose. In all long periods of time it is difficult to get accurate estimates, for the year is not a constant unit.

Past races have used different calendar systems, and the only constant unit of time is that of the Daniel

TREASURE OF OPHIR

Cycle. In that system a very long astronomical period is employed, so that its unit is a constant one. It owes its name to the fact that the prophet Daniel seems to have discovered and employed it. While it would be very difficult to attempt any accurate estimates, a rough approximation of dates helps us to appreciate some of the details of Genesis history which can be expanded with present-day knowledge, until it is shown to be very precise and accurate.

After the tribe left Eden we are left to fill in the minor details of bedou life, and we next meet the Adamites as a settled tribe, leading the type of life that geographical conditions have imposed on the Arabs and on many inhabitants of Iraq districts. I use Arab comparisons, for Arabia and Arab-speaking peoples inhabit the lands that are nearest to the Basin Valley which those prediluvian tribes peopled. Before the Great Flood the river Euphrates flowed east of its present outlet, Fao. Its outlet was the Indian Ocean, and not a Basin Valley which was later inundated.

CHAPTER IV

THE RED RACE

GENESIS shows the headman Adam and his wife Eve in their settled homestead. This Adam was not necessarily the same headman who led his people out of the Aden oasis, and the advanced state of civilization which is described suggests that history has been resumed many hundred years after the exodus from Eden. This is the Adam from whom tribal genealogy is first dated, and the genealogy is a very wonderful one, for it gives tribal dates from the first family known to history, and onward to times that come within the scope of civil history.

The Sheikh Adam, head of the Red Race, and his family were living the life that is typical of an oasis sheikh of the present day. Life among the semi-nomads helps me to appreciate many details of the story of that family—details which must be somewhat obscure to Western knowledge.

The names of Adam's two sons were in all probability post-mortem ones, for they are peculiarly fitting to their lives, and such descriptions could hardly have been accidents of birth. The name of the first-born was

TREASURE OF OPHIR

Cain, which may have meant the Chosen One or Heir, or may be a derivative from the Hebrew word Qayin, Spear or Lance. At first sight Qayin seems to be the meaning of Cain, but later in the history we find that Chosen One is a more likely interpretation. Perhaps the name was a punning one, having a double meaning. It is generally accepted that Abel meant Vanity, in which case it probably was a post-mortem title.

Cain served his apprenticeship on the land, and became shiekh of the fields. Abel had the somewhat harder lot of sheikh of the live-stock. Under normal conditions the family would have grown up in the homestead till that home became uncomfortably crowded. Then the eldest son, Cain, and not the second, Abel, would have taken his wife, family, retinue and as much property as Sheikh Adam would spare, and wandered off and formed his own tribe, a sub-tribe of the Adamites. Abel would have succeeded his father, and dropped his own name, adopting his father's title, and thus becoming the new Sheikh Adam, head of the Adam tribe. If, on the other hand, the Adam home had not been overcrowded, then Cain would have succeeded his father and in all probability both the names Cain and Abel would have been lost to history.

But a drought occurred and upset the even tenor of their tribal life, and here I can call upon personal experience gained when living among oasis Arabs to reconstruct the action which followed. At the

THE RED RACE

commencement of the year the husbandmen are busy building dykes and banks to catch the flow of the flood stream which will come with the spring rains. The herdsmen have to take their flocks afar, for winter pasturage is scarce. When the rain fails the husbandmen have the hard work of trying to save the crops by digging shallow wells to catch all surface moisture, and ladling it out with leather buckets to save such small crops as they have raised.

The herdsmen's worst difficulties come later in the year, when they have to kill off a large proportion of their stock, so that their lessened pasturage shall support their diminished flocks. In the autumn season of a drought year, skins and hides are plentiful, owing to the slaughter of the flock weaklings. With that knowledge we can appreciate the conditions in this year of famine.

Throughout the long summer Cain had hard work and great anxiety trying to save his scanty crops. Abel had harder work than under normal conditions, since he had to roam farther in search of pasturage, but of the two Cain had by far the more anxious time.

Consequently at the autumn harvest thanksgiving, which is common to all agricultural peoples, Abel could well afford to contribute "the firstlings of the flock and the fat thereof". Meanwhile the shrinking pastures had forced graminivorous wild life to seek other feeding grounds. The wild goat, gazelle, desert hare, wild camel, and ass moved off to other oases. But the carnivorous wild life was closing in, extracting heavy toll from the weakened graminivorous fauna.

Kite, vulture, fox, jackal, hyena, and wild cat were preying on the remnants of the starving animals who had held to their homes, hoping that the famine would break. Now, while starved and weakened, they tried to force their way through the ring of carnivorous animals that were growing strong in their plentiful hunting grounds.

The day of thanksgiving dawned and the two brothers, sheikh of the fields and sheikh of the flocks, took their thankofferings to the palm grove that served them as temple. It is fair to presume that they went to the grove at sunrise, for that is the time that the working day starts, and we have fair indication that the Adamites were sun worshippers, or that their religion was closely connected with sun worship.

No altar is mentioned, so it is evident that they laid their offerings on the ground, and, after a few simple prayers, departed. Meanwhile the kite and vulture were wheeling their ceaseless patrol overhead in a sky which was losing the hues of dawn and hardening to the metallic blue of a tropical day. From every shrub there peeped the hungry eyes of desert hare, rat, and field mouse. A rustle in the desert heather, and a jerboah rat, weak with hunger, tottered toward the pile of vegetables, which was Cain's offerings, but almost before the jerboah had buried its teeth in a head of millet grain there was a pounce, and a wild cat had

THE RED RACE

taken its toll. A rustle of wings, and a hawk swept swiftly by in vain hope of robbing the wild cat of its prey.

A whistle in the blue overhead told that a kite was calling to his mate. Away in the heights a speck appeared and grew larger as a white vulture swooped down toward the heap of dead meat that represented Abel's offering. That speck in the sky was replaced by another watcher, and soon the pile of meat was covered with vultures.

Throughout the day vulture and wild dog quarrelled over the spoil, the vultures gaining most of the feast, the dogs only darting in when the vultures were heavy and less watchful. I have watched such a scene, where the carrion feeders gorged throughout the whole day, and left at eventide only a few morsels for the night prowlers to clean from the stripped skeleton.

When the Adamites returned at sunset the offering of Abel showed only as a pile of gleaming bones, while a bundle of withered green stuff seemed to show that the god of the Adamites had no respect for the offerings of Cain.

It is so easy to understand the jeering and the ceaseless taunts of Abel, whose rivalry had met with such signal victory.

The tragedy that occurred was the outcome of a quarrel between two hot-blooded men, but afterwards the eldest brother must have faced life in its most hellish

TREASURE OF OPHIR

aspects. Though a fratricide, he could not leave the family circle, for the desert will not support a man unaided. He could not go off with tribal property, for without his father's support he would have been killed by the friends of Abel. At length satisfactory arrangements were made with a bedou tribe, and it is evident that Cain took full tribal retinue and property with him, for he rose to prominence in the tribe that adopted him. It has been suggested that this tribe from the Land of Wanderers was a Mongol tribe, which suggestion gives satisfactory explanation.

Then follows a genealogy which is seemingly the most amazing one on record, simply because tribal customs are not generally understood in the West. Adam had a third son, Seth, and later had further sons and daughters who are not named. But an Arab sheikh will often allude to all his dependants as his sons and daughters, for in his household all are treated alike.

"Adam lived a hundred and thirty years", though we should note that the prediluvian year was three hundred and sixty days, and not three hundred and sixty-five days of the present reckoning. That age is a long one, but by no means impossible, for I have met a sheikh who was certainly one hundred and thirteen years old, and he claimed that he was ten years older. He requested me to give him a potent tonic, as he was not feeling his best and he intended to marry a girl of sixteen. I succeeded in dissuading him from that

THE RED RACE

venture, only to find that his virility got him into serious trouble at Aden some three months later.

Whilst Adam lived to 130, his tribe lasted another 800 years, and Seth set up his own tribe. The full tribal genealogy is recorded on these lines. At times the genealogy offers difficulties regarding the minor age. For instance, it is stated that the Jared lived 162 years, while the full length of the Jared tribe was 962 years. That does not necessarily mean that the individual patriarch Jared lived 162 years, and such a suggestion would seem improbable. It does show that the Jared tribe continued some 162 years before the offshoot Enoch tribe was formed.

Again, there is somewhat puzzling information regarding the Enoch tribe, who disappeared after 365 years. It has been suggested that this number 365 is mythical, and has some allusion to the number of days in a year. But that suggestion falls to the ground when we remember that the 365-day year is quite a modern institution. In all probability the Enoch tribe were lost in the desert, being overtaken by sandstorms, or perhaps perishing through lack of water after losing their way to the wells for which they were heading.

Different versions of Genesis give different age estimates, so we can only regard the numbers as approximate, though the records were very carefully kept at the time. We note the accuracy when we come to the link between prediluvian and post-diluvian genealogies.

TREASURE OF OPHIR

Here we find there is apparently a gap of two years between the two genealogies. When we look into Flood history we note that the tribes in question had joined up with the Noah tribe during their stay in the Ark, and that accounts for the two-year gap in a genealogy that is continuous for more than 1,600 years of the earliest record of humanity.

CHAPTER V

THE FATE OF A NATION

THE Flood era has been subjected to a great deal of destructive criticism, and to very little constructive criticism. It contains the main deductions by which we find the River Pison, so we need to look into it somewhat closely, and we then find that the Flood era is the best substantiated of all Genesis history. It is a history of oceans, storms, and ships, but we find that the destructive criticisms have been written by landsmen who are not qualified to examine that type of evidence, which belongs to the peculiar province of the trained seaman. It is with the outlook of a trained seaman that I examined the evidence of the Flood and found its convincing truths.

The year of the Flood is termed *Anno Mundi*, for it marked the commencement of a new world. We are not entirely dependent on Genesis accounts for details of the Flood, for there are Flood legends throughout the world. Some of those legends may refer to local catastrophes which were not connected with the Biblical Flood and Deluge, but when we compare all available evidence it becomes fairly certain that most of the legends refer to the same event, an event that was world-wide—a catastrophe quite as appalling as the Hebrew chroniclers have related.

The Adamite race had long anticipated disaster, and attributed its causes to "The Cursing of the Ground", which occurred more than 1536 years earlier. An anticipation of more than 1,500 years suggests that the cause of the Flood was an astronomical one, and the evidence of Flood legends supports that suggestion, as does the presence of the thistle, to which we drew attention in earlier pages. The thistle is mainly a plant of temperate climates.

I do not as yet postulate the acceptance of the Basin Valley theories. The evidence of those theories is cumulative, but the location of the Adamites is already fairly definite, for the Euphrates was one of the rivers of the Eden river-junction. In the Euphrates Valley of the present time the thistle is hardly known, and does not exist in sufficient prominence to be emphasized as one of the hindrances which would impede the Adamites after their exodus from Eden. "Cursed is the ground. . . . Thorns and thistles shall it bring forth. . . . In the sweat of thy face shalt thou eat bread. . . ." Those are the conditions that the Adamites faced some 1,500 or 2,000 years after their exodus from Eden.

The earth was rocking on its axis, and the latitude of their home was changing. Geology shows us that this change of latitude had occurred many times

THE FATE OF A NATION

previously in the geological ages. The Northern Polar cap was slipping toward the equator of the eastern longitude. Consequently the Adamite home was growing steadily colder, and in succeeding years even a primitive race would have had no difficulty in noting that there was a change of latitude.

It is, however, very illogical to assume that the Adamites were a primitive race. There is no mention throughout their long history of any wars or civil disturbances until 2600 B.C., when the civil wars of their lands are duly recorded. Their histories had been kept intact for countless ages, and had been very definite for 1,500 years. That shows a land under settled conditions.

Successive civilizations borrow remarkably little from their predecessors. Fifteen hundred years of undisturbed progress should have given them a very advanced civilization, though that progress may well have been on different lines to the progress of European and American civilization.

Granted that their latitude changed steadily, we should still find that most of their progress was made in a torrid or moderately torrid zone, where the night skies are more clear than in our temperate zones. Surely they reached a very high stage in astronomical science. Observations for latitude are amongst the easiest of astronomical observations, for they require no precise time notation. Without any astronomical instrument other than a stone cairn or a stick, these people could have taken accurate observations for latitude. They had no difficulty in seeing that their latitude was changing, and that their lands would inevitably be inundated by the waters that came pouring from the north during the winter seasons, when the north monsoon wind was blowing. If that was so, we are faced with the query: "Why did they not leave their lands and seek some place of safety?"

The answer is obvious. They did not leave because they could not leave. Their religion, and therefore their political organization, was based on the principle of a Personal God, of whom they were the chosen race, and the "only" race. Their leaders, such as Adam, Enoch, and Lamech, were "sons of God". In distinction their neighbours were heathen, and, not being the chosen of their God, they were mere "sons and daughters of men". Their first tribal law had brought a result which, in all probability, they had not anticipated.

By that law the man had to join the wife's tribe, and that discouraged any marriage outside the man's tribe, for if he chose a "foreign" wife, he took his property away, and his own people were weakened, both in man-power and in tribal property. By 2600 B.C. the full disadvantages of the system were apparent. Politically they were isolated, and the Adamites commenced to break down that isolation. Consanguinity had played havoc with the Adamite tribes, and their attempts to adjust matters were too late to gain success.

THE FATE OF A NATION

The immediate result of a widened marriage sphere was excellent, for the union with non-Adamite tribes brought "giants in those days", and "mighty men which were of old men of renown". That could not save the Adamites, for they were penned into a Basin Valley, and they could not break through the hill ranges. The valley was filled with disturbance and violence among their own tribes, so they could not combine sufficiently to break through the hills. The hills contained tribes who had only sufficient to support themselves, and would certainly resent any invasion from the lowland tribes of the Basin Valley.

THE BASIN VALLEY
All land over 4,000 feet is shown as Mountain Chains

In this Basin Valley the Euphrates flowed to a river junction with three other rivers. Later came the great Flood, which altered the whole face of the land, and

TREASURE OF OPHIR

changed the river courses. The Hiddekel was probably the Tigris, which did not join the Euphrates at its present junction of Mohammerah, the head of the Shatt el Arab. In the prediluvian days the Hiddekel flowed from the Tigris on through the bed of the Bahmaseer, parallel to the Euphrates, then eastward through the Basin Valley, and to the river junction, which was somewhere in the latitude of Fao and the longitude of Bahrein.

There the Euphrates and Hiddekel were met by the Pison, which is now the Wadi Dawasir, and "compasseth the whole land of Havilah", the land for which we are searching. The fourth river was the Gihon, that flowed from the river junction onward and eastward to its sea outlet at Ras Mussandam. This Gihon compassed the whole land of Aethiopia, but not the Aethiopia of the present day, which is better known as Abyssinia. The Gihon compassed the Muscat territories of the Oman province, the land of the Black Arabs, who later moved south and occupied Abyssinia, giving to their new colony the ethnological distincton of Aethiopia.

Their ancient forefathers remained in Oman, and their descendants are a black negroid race, Aethiopians in fact, who are ethnologically distinct from the fair-skinned Semitic Arabs.

These Aethiopians of Arabia gave their name Aethiopia to Abyssinia many centuries after the coming of the Flood.

CHAPTER VI

THE FLOOD

THE Adamites made their exit from Eden in an easterly direction, and when once they had abandoned any attempts at return, their settlements blocked any further tribes from turning in a westerly direction, and so set the flow of tribal migration in an easterly direction, till the whole Basin Valley was filled. The last of the main Adamite tribes was the Noah, and to the Noah were attached the three offshoot tribes—Shem, Ham, and Japhet. Undoubtedly they occupied the creeks of Ras Mussandam.

The Noah was a shipbuilding tribe, and from their commencement it was their tradition that the Noah would find the deliverance that was anticipated as the final outcome of the Curse of the Ground. Their surprising shipbuilding ability puts them near the sea coast in Euphrates latitudes, and we are furnished with further evidence which helps to localize them more exactly. Their sagacity during the Flood period shows that they would have been fully cognizant of the rainbow, if they had been in a land where a rainbow could be seen.

The creeks of Massandam are deep-water creeks,

though they were probably some ten fathoms more shallow in prediluvian days. At present they are too hot for human habitation, but in those days of more temperate climate they may have been very pleasant localities. They were tidal or semi-tidal regions, and their river outlet made them ideal for shipbuilding. The creeks are precipitous rock clefts, and their horizon is very constricted. A rainbow necessitates an horizon of low altitude, and land or sea sufficiently cool for cloud diffusion to afford the refraction that makes a rainbow. In those rocky headlands it is unlikely that a rainbow would form, and certainly a rainbow could not have been seen, since their outlook was never to distant levels.

Here in the creeks of Ras Massandam the Noah could note the increasing tidal ranges, and with the coming of the north monsoon floods and rains, could see that the inundation of the Basin Valley was inevitable. While astronomy gave the causes and the reasons to anticipate disaster, they had daily evidence that catastrophe must overwhelm their world, and one hundred and twenty years before the flood the Noah made their definite preparations. They adopted a policy of isolation, for they considered that they only were righteous.

There is a theory that the Genesis account of the Flood is an exaggeration of an annual occurrence that takes place. The theory has been held amongst European residents in Mesopotamia for several years, and it

THE FLOOD

has lately been published in England, where it created some sensation and was generally accepted. The suggestion is, that on one occasion the annual flood of the Euphrates was greater than anticipated, and in consequence some loss of life occurred, which disaster has been magnified by tradition, and has been incorporated in Genesis as the history of the Flood and Deluge.

I am able to state definitely and categorically that the Minor Flood theory is incorrect. It has been worked out with care, and the interest it has aroused may prove beneficial. In these days it is very difficult to persuade an educated person to give any serious attention to Genesis history, and the latest author of the Minor Flood theory deserves the fullest congratulation on his achievement; but if he had enjoyed my more extended and wider opportunities for investigation, he would have learned where the Minor Flood theory exhibits fallacies that render it untenable.

All the Genesis evidence prior to the date of the Flood is against a Minor Flood theory; and that evidence is ignored by the supporters of that theory. The suggestion that succeeding evidence is exaggerated by tradition is absolutely discounted when we consider the circumstances of construction and the actual measurements of that surprisingly great ship, the Ark-Gopher, popularly known as the Ark.

The Noah at this time had more than 1,400 years of civilization behind them, and ages of experience in building river craft. The geographical conditions of their land, with its sheltered river waters to west, and its open ocean to east, gave them ideal opportunities for progressing in the art of seamanship.

The trade winds gave them every encouragement to practice all the arts of navigation, so that it would be surprising if they were not as well advanced in shipbuilding and in navigation as the British of to-day; for the British have in 1,500 years progressed from an initial stage that was probably inferior to that of the prediluvians, and any shipbuilding that they learned from earlier races was a hindrance, not a help. At the present date shipbuilders have not progressed far beyond a tonnage of 44,000 tons gross.

That seems to have been about the tonnage of the ship which the Noah took some hundred and twenty years to design and build. We rely on the estimates of former investigators, who give 42,413 tons gross. It has been suggested that the original measurements of the Ark have been exaggerated, and that Genesis gives the exaggerated estimates, but any exaggeration would have been very difficult, and is, in fact, very unlikely. The Genesis measurements are in excellent proportion, and the suggestion that they are a multiplication does not hold. For instance, if the measurements have been multiplied several times, then the original measurements contained fractions of a cubit.

It is usual to speak of this ship as The Ark. Accurately speaking, she should be called the Ark-Gopher. The phrase in the Authorised Version of the Old

CROSSING THE TIGRIS IN A GOPHER

Facing page 187]

THE FLOOD

Testament runs: "Make thee an ark of gopher wood", but no one has discovered, nor will they discover, what "gopher wood" is, for it does not, and never did, exist.

The phrase should evidently read: "Make thee an Ark-Gopher of wood", for translation of the original version would allow that adjustment, and it gives full meaning to a command that would otherwise have been impossible. *You cannot build a ship of only one kind of timber.* Short-grained wood is required for the knees and framing, which take the supporting strains. Long-grained timber is requisite for the longitudinals, skin and deck plating.

"Gopher" is still the name employed on the Euphrates for the circular craft which are built of bent timbers, such as the various incense gum woods. They are woven with wattles, and then pitched within and without with native bitumen. The Ark was a giant river craft of unique design. She was a "Gopher", or river craft, but she was Ark, or box-like, in her lines. She was three-decked, with cabins, and with a roof that was probably turtle-backed. To this covering she had a window, or what we should call a trap hatch. This giant ship had only one gangway, or "door".

It is very doubtful whether modern shipbuilders could build a wooden ship of that size and design, for now that we have abandoned wood for first-class shipbuilding we should find the calculations of strain and material very difficult and intricate. The Ark was probably built mainly of mahogany and dwarf oak.

TREASURE OF OPHIR

It is absurd to suggest that this ship was designed for a family of under twenty people. A family so small could not have tended all the live-stock they had aboard, and certainly four men could not have undertaken the building of a ship of over 40,000 tons. The ship was built for one main tribe, the Noah, and for the three sub-tribes—Shem, Ham, and Japhet. If this great ship was built, there must have been many other first-class ships afloat. The Chinese suggestion no longer seems absurd; they probably have prediluvian designs in their Northern junks.

The suggestion of early world-wide navigation is strengthened by the Assyrian Flood records, which are very interesting, though they are greatly inferior to Genesis records. Assyrian legends mention wind and thunder in the shape of gods, and they ascribe great credit to the master-navigator of the ship which we call the Ark.

While building the Ark, the Noah worked out all the intricate details of provisioning and accommodation of animals and personnel. They appear to have taken great trouble to ensure the balance of Nature in the drowned world which they rightly anticipated they should face. They first decided to take pairs of every sort of bird, animal, and reptile, together with the necessary food for their provision. They probably took about three hundred species of mammalia and five hundred species of bird life.

That estimate is a rough one, for if they were under

THE FLOOD

different climatic conditions to the present day, their zoology was different to that of the present day. They can have had little difficulty in collecting their species, for floods were periodical, and during flood periods animals and birds are in a cowed state. They classified their animals as clean and unclean. Probably the graminivorous faunæ were considered clean, while the carnivorous, being offal-eaters in almost every case, were considered unclean animals. Later calculations showed sufficient accommodation for seven pairs of each clean animal, whilst the unclean were kept to the original number, namely, one pair of each species.

This decision seems to have been made only seven days before the commencement of the Deluge, and at the final embarkation of the Noah tribes. Perhaps they had kept spare accommodation for refugees, and now decided to utilize that spare deck space. *Anno Mundi*, the year of the Flood Deluge is difficult to determine, and estimates range between 4000 B.C., or even earlier, and 2400 B.C., as about the latest possible estimate. We have employed 2480 B.C. as the standard, because that seems the latest probable date that will fit in with other evidence.

Whilst *Anno Mundi* is indeterminate, we have a great deal of evidence to show that the calendar date of the Flood was November 1st. There are Flood legends from all over the world, including Assyria, several parts of India, Polynesia, North America, Mexico, Greece, Southern Arabia, and, of course, Mount Ararat districts.

TREASURE OF OPHIR

The little-known South Arabian legends are particularly interesting, for they suggest that the whole Rift Valley, from the head of the Red Sea to the eastern end of the Gulf of Aden, was dry land in prediluvian days. If that was so, it gives the solution to the puzzle of why there are no Flood legends in Egypt; for the flooding of the Rift Valley would have absorbed the waters sufficiently to have preserved Egypt from serious inundation.

In the Basin Valley latitudes the Northern monsoon sets in during October. So, early in October, we presume the Noah, Shem, Ham, and Japhet tribes assembled near to their Ark-Gopher, awaiting the command of their leader to embark. They of course left everything portable to the last moment, and their final embarkation was completed about October 25th. The ship was not yet launched, and they needed to be careful to give her no unnecessary strain while she still lay in her cradle, or on her building ground. Despite her immense size, she seems to have been very lightly built, for it was necessary to pitch her within and without. With the tide races and flood currents it would have been extremely unwise to float so huge a craft before it was necessary to do so.

The Flood and Deluge commenced. The succeeding details enable us to construct a Flood Calendar, and November 1st fits in very accurately for its commencement. Polynesian legends say that the Flood rose as the sun approached the horizon. In Hawaii the Flood was

THE FLOOD

called the Flood of the Moon. Some legends connect the Flood with volcanic outbreak, but cumulative evidence suggests that the Flood was caused by some astronomical effect, and resulted in a huge tidal wave that travelled over most of the globe.

If the Flood commenced at sunrise at Hawaii, then we can allow for difference in apparent time, and for the time which the main tidal wave took to travel. That will give sunset as the time the Flood burst through the Straits of Ras Mussandam. According to Hebrew chronology, sunset is the commencement of the day. Babylonian records support the suggestion of sunset for Flood commencement, since they allude to "the splendour of sunset".

Picture the scene, for it is well worth an effort of imagination. The rising flood had by this time lifted the Ark from her cradle, and the Noah had warped her out to the open waters of the river Gihon, for no seaman would have dreamed of keeping his ship in enclosed waters at such a time, so in the main stream the Ark-Gopher lay straining at her hawsers, which stretched bar taut to the muddy waters. She looked like a giant black sea slug chained to the river bed.

To the north of her was a lowering drift of dark cloud, with now and then a break in it where cloud scud broke and raced to leeward. All around her was flying spume and to southward the horizon was blotted out by rain mist. Whenever the sunlight did break through it showed as a sickly copper hue. The wind

TREASURE OF OPHIR

changed from steady north-westerly breeze to swift hurricane gale. All animal life was hushed, cowed with expectancy of disaster, and as the wind increased to an overwhelming roar, conversation died out in the gloomy 'tween decks.

The water whipped into waves of a curious pyramid formation, while the Ark-Gopher bobbed and danced at her hawsers. This was encouraging, for it showed that the ship was light and lively in accord with her design. Suddenly there was an ominous lull, and the seamen glanced at each other with fright in their eyes. It was the lull before the definite break of the greatest storm in history. The sailors had faced many a hurricane, but never such a storm as this lull presaged. A dull roaring came to them with swift and ever-increasing volume.

"The fountains of the great deep", murmured the Sheikh Noah, he whom the Assyrians called Puzur Bel, the Master Navigator.

The great hawsers creaked, then with a whip, snap and hiss they parted like cotton threads. The ship rode easy, then next moment she rose, up and up, until, with a noise like thunder, the first tidal wave broke right over her. How could the puny efforts of man override these great forces of Nature? Yet, after a time that seemed like eternity, the Ark-Gopher rose, climbed and dipped to each great sea that came sweeping through the gate of Ormuz.

From here onwards the Flood narrative of Genesis

THE FLOOD

reads like a ship's log, penned by the hand of that Master Navigator, the great Noah himself. We need no imagination, for the record is clear and convincing.

Down came the Deluge, rain continued unceasingly until December 11th. If there were any ships that had survived the bursting of the Flood, they were soon filled, their food destroyed, and their cordage rotted, so that no life could have been aboard them. The Deluge and Flood caused a permanent displacement of ocean level. All known land was covered to a depth of $22\frac{1}{2}$ feet. The Flood is mentioned apart from the Deluge, and it seems that the Flood stream set in from the termination of the Deluge for forty days. That brings the culmination of the Flood stream to January 21st.

The Persian Gulf of the present day is surrounded by mountains, some of which are over 9,000 feet above sea levels. As those mountains were covered, the crew of the Ark concluded that all life was extinct. Certainly all life of the Adamite world was drowned. How did the crew of the Ark know where they were? They had lived in a world of mountains, valleys, rock gorges, rivers, forests, and teeming life. Now, as they floated on a weary waste of waters, how were they to know the depth to which their highest mountain peaks were covered?

With the tidal wave-burst they were carried westward, then south-westward, since the Flood stream was from the north. During the forty days of Deluge they can have sighted no land with which to gain land bearings and judge their position and the course of the currents. Further, they can have taken no astronomical sights during that time, when all the Heavenly bodies were hidden by rainfall. Under such conditions the most skilful navigator might well lose all reckoning of his position. Yet these old navigators knew their whereabouts so accurately that they could say the shoalest depths were $22\frac{1}{2}$ feet.

The Flood ceased to rise, and the Ark grounded on Ararat, March 31st. From then onward there was a steady fall of Flood waters, and by June 13th the tops of the mountains began to appear. These dates are taken from November 1st as the standard date; calculating with thirty-day months, this gives the fall of the Flood at about the change of the monsoon, which is what we should expect. The first showing of the mountain-tops was when the south monsoon had well set in, and its winds were driving the waters back to northward.

By July 23rd the fine weather had set in, so the top hatch was opened and two birds were loosed. The raven is a bird of strong flight and a scavenger. Its return would show that the Flood waters had not yet receded to habitable level. Its absence showed that the raven had found offal, and therefore the level where animal life could be maintained. The dove—for this was, in all probability, the plum-coloured palm dove—is of weaker flight, and would seek lower levels. Its absence would show that sufficiently low level had been

THE FLOOD

reached for vegetation, and therefore for the tribes to grow their grain.

The raven did not return to the Ark, and when the dove returned it was evident that, though habitable land had been found for animals, there were not sufficient low levels for grain growing. The crew were able to observe the rate of tide fall, and seven days later, about July 30th, the dove was again freed. It returned with an olive leaf, probably for nesting, and this gave all requisite information. The level of the olive trees had been reached, but that is not necessarily the level of the date palm, and of the plains.

On August 6th the dove was freed again, and this time did not return. Its absence showed that the lowlands were drying, and there would be good soil for the crops. Moreover, the date harvest would be greatly improved by the long submersion of the date palms. Safety was in sight, but there would be no sense in abandoning the Ark before the lowlands were well dried, drained, and thoroughly warmed. On the other hand, the crew urgently needed a catch crop so as to have some fresh food for their livestock.

On September 11th the Flood had entirely receded, the south monsoon was in full force, they had a month or more to dry out their ship, recaulk her, and make all necessary repairs in preparation for the anniversary and possible return of the Flood. Their astronomers were now able to take accurate sights, which determined their astronomical position, while careful triangulation gave them their geographical position.

It is certain they did this intricate work, for after this series of observations, and after they left the Ark on November 6th, the astronomers were definitely able to assure them that there would never be another catastrophic Flood.

By very accurate observation of latitude they could tell that the change of earth axis had passed its culmination point. Necessarily their astronomy was of very high order, for, though the refraction had changed, they were able to make the necessary adjustment to their observations.

Starting a new life in the lands of their origin, they saw the wide horizons for the first time. The rainbow was a new phenomena to the tribes, and was regarded as a symbol of safety from future Flood. The Flood narrative shows a wealth of detail superior to any mythical tale. Its history reads like extracts from the carefully prepared ship's log, or the note-book of a first-class navigator. It shows the Flood approaching and receding, according to monsoon changes. It shows that the rate of rise and fall were very carefully observed. Indeed, it shows a race who were very knowledgeable in navigation, astronomy, natural history, and in botanical science. This scientific race, who had survived their cruise in the Ark-Gopher, handed down their sciences to succeeding tribes, among which we may include the Tribe of Ophir.

CHAPTER VII

THE LAND OF OPHIR

Now that we have the Flood narrative placed on an intelligent historical basis, we can examine the evidence so far as it concerns our problem. It is evident that the Flood did occur, and was of large magnitude. It swept through the Straits of Ormuz, and submerged the River Gihon. It swept onward, and, meeting the Euphrates and Hiddekel flowing in contrary direction, it changed their river courses somewhat, whilst also submerging the Eastern portions of their river-beds. Consequently they now have a junction at the head of the Shatt el Arab and their common outlet is at Fao. But the River Pison flowed at right angles to the trend of the Flood tidal-wave. So the bed of the Pison was covered with debris and is now subterranean, though its course is still shown by the Wadi Dawasir.

We shall find the Land of Havilah compassed by the Wadi Dawasir, and when we have found Havilah we shall be able to trace out the other two lands, Jobab and Ophir. In the tribal history that follows the Flood narrative we learn how the sons of Joktan, Havilah, Jobab and Ophir came to their lands.

TREASURE OF OPHIR

In the Ararat country there was a tribal gathering, probably an anniversary feast to commemorate their deliverance from the Flood. Noah, the Head Sheikh, got drunk, and the Sheikh of Ham tried to make political gain out of the incident. The Sheikhs of Shem and Japhet refused to support the political ambitions of the Sheikh of Ham and preserved their loyalty to the Noah. Noah promptly called a tribal meeting, or durbar, and gave his judgment on the matter. He called the Japhet to alliance with the Shem, and he definitely elected the Shem as tribal leader next in seniority to Noah. With this alliance of Shem and Ham, and with the full support of Noah, the Ham were absolutely and permanently subjugated. "Cursed be Canaan," said Noah, and, as Cain meant heir, Canaan, the plural, referred to the heirs of Ham.

It is impossible to suppose that a sprightly old gentleman of some six hundred years got intensely intoxicated and then woke with such virility and clear thought that he issued a curse which has re-echoed through the ages. Further, if one chooses such an interpretation, one is apt to feel that he might have cursed the right man, instead of letting his wrath fall on Canaan for an indiscretion that was committed by Ham, the father of Canaan. All absurdities vanish when we realize that the historical incident mainly refers to tribes and to the headmen of those tribes.

Wherever the Ham tribe colonized they were later driven out or subjugated by the tribal combination. In

THE LAND OF OPHIR

the temperate climates they were so subjugated that there is no trace of them. They tried the Hami or hot lands, but as soon as they had undertaken all the difficult work of pioneering, the more virile Shem came and dispossessed the ennervated Ham of their lands. The Ham colonized all the Persian Gulf Coasts of Southern Arabia, but inevitably they were followed up and their lands taken from them by the Semitic races. They worked further east, as their prediluvian forefathers had done, and we find some traces of them, though we are unable to distinguish them from the later negroids and Hamites who have been imported as slaves from Sudan and North Africa. From Arabia they crossed over to Abyssinia, only to meet the same fate in due course.

We can trace this same fate following the Hamites through many lands, but for our purpose we need only to note that they were chased from Oman and the Hasa, their original Aethiopia, down through Yemen and Assir, and so overseas to Abyssinia. South Arabia was first peopled by the Ham, who were later succeeded by the Semitic "sons of Joktan".

In Southern Arabia the Wadi Dawasir compasseth, or forms, an eastern boundary round a land which I identify as Havilah. That intrepid Arabian explorer, Edouard Glaser, lived in the northern lands of the Wadi Dawasir, and he identified the Wadi Dawasir as the River Pison. I lived at the southern extremity of the Wadi Dawasir, used entirely different methods to those of Glaser, of whose investigations I had no knowledge,

199

TREASURE OF OPHIR

and came to the same conclusion. We both identify the Wadi Dawasir as the lost River Pison. The land it "compasseth" is Assir and Northern Yemen, which is the land I shall identify as Havilah.

Following further south and eastward comes the

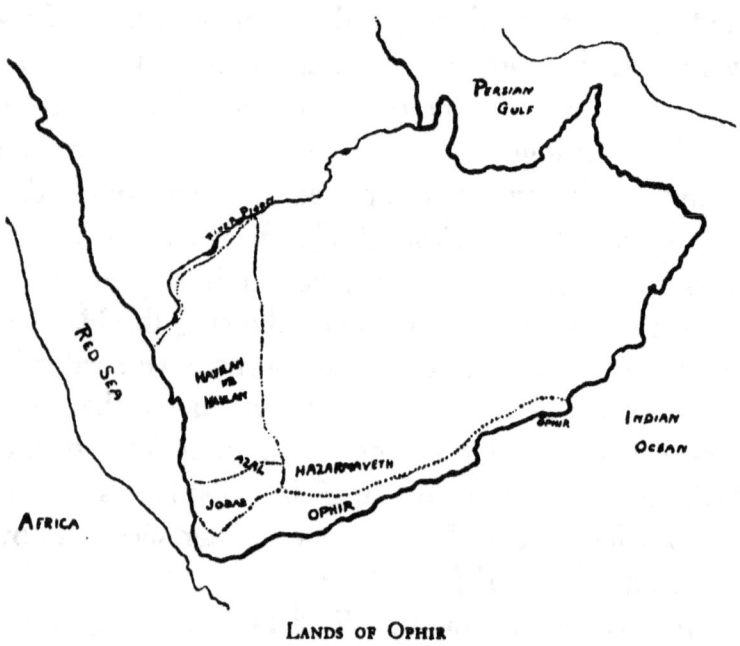

LANDS OF OPHIR

next geographical division, which starts from the district of Ibb in Yemen and stretches down to the northern boundaries of the Aden Protectorate, that is, the land of Jobab. Then come the coastal plains as far east as the Dhofar district, that is, the Beled Ophir, or, in the

THE LAND OF OPHIR

plural, Beled Ophar, the land of the Ophir tribes, whose gophers plied the coast to Mesha, the port I shall show.

Here are the proofs of those assertions, entirely in accord with the local tribal evidence:

"In the land of Havilah there is gold, bdellium, and the onyx stone," says Genesis.

In Assir and Northern Yemen there certainly is gold. Personally, I have only located three of those ancient gold-mines, but a Turkish explorer who has travelled all through Northern Yemen tells me of the gold there. Summarized, his evidence would read: "There is gold, and the gold of that land is good."

On one of my visits to Assir the sheikhs of the hinterland heard that I had some knowledge of minerals, and sent down messages asking me to come and develop their gold territories. My host, the late Seyidt Mahomedt Idrissi, assured me that the gold is certainly there, but he advised me not to go after it, because he could not guarantee my safety if I went into the interior, since the tribesmen are somewhat fanatical. If I did return, he did not think I should bring back any of the gold of Havilah. One of those Assir districts is still known as Haulan, which seems a modern rendering of Havilah in its dual plural. From what I can gather, it seems that the natives have cleaned off the surface outcrops, but have been unable to proceed further in their mining because they cannot blast and have no knowledge of machinery.

There is no reasonable doubt that Assir and

TREASURE OF OPHIR

Northern Yemen hold gold, so I turned my attention to the next evidence regarding Havilah. "There is bdellium and the onyx stone." Bdellium is an unknown substance. Glaser suggested that bdellium might be gum-arabic, but gum-arabic would seem rather out of place, being a vegetable substance, sandwiched in between two mineral locations.

Others have suggested pearls. But there are no rivers of South Arabia sufficiently large to yield river pearls, and sea pearls could not exist in the Land of Havilah, though they might exist off its shores. If bdellium were the pearl, it would offer no satisfactory location for Havilah, since there are pearl-banks all round the coasts of Arabia. The onyx stone offered no more certain clue, for it seems that the Biblical onyx might include agates, cornelians and indeed, any kind of low-grade carborundum.

When I stayed at Azal I had no difficulty in finding both the bdellium and the onyx stone. Merchants came with many semi-precious stones, and while arranging for their purchase I inquired where each stone came from. Among these stones were found agates of every colour, and plenty of true onyx; also a curious stone that is a type of high-grade marble, so ornamental that it serves well for necklaces and semi-precious jewellery.

By mapping out the places from which these stones were obtained I found three different strata. The gold land lays to the north of Havilah; the semi-precious marble which I identify as bdellium lies to the south

THE LAND OF OPHIR

of the gold land, and the onyx, which includes both true and Biblical onyx, is in the southern strata. The whole land is compassed by the Wadi Dawasir, which Glaser has already identified as the River Pison and which I also have identified as the same lost river.

I claim that Havilah is identified. Now for Jobab.

"There was a man of Uz called Job." Job is the individual name of the tribal term Jobab, where "ab" means "father". Job was a "man of Uz", of Azal on his mother's side, and he was a man of Jobab on his father's side. I write these notes at Azal, and the natives all consider that Job is a patriarch of their lands. Geographical conditions, with their mountain ranges, suggest that Azal is the northern boundary of the Jobab country. The modern name of Azal is Sanaa, and it is the capital of Yemen. There is only one mention of Jobab in Genesis, and there is no other mention of the name in Hebrew records to guide us in the locality of Jobab. However, a study of the locality makes it fairly certain that the Jobab were a tribe of Southern Yemen and probably in the lands due south of Azal.

With Havilah and Jobab located, we now take the ancient caravan route that existed in Genesis days and is still in use. Starting in the north from Jerah, which Mr. Philby has rightly identified as Oqair of the Qatar Peninsula, we travel down through Havilah and Jobab, then turn sharply to the east, leaving the main territories of Hazarmaveth to north of us. Hazarmaveth ("In the presence of Death") received its name because its

TREASURE OF OPHIR

northern boundaries skirt the dead lands of the Ruba l Kali, or Empty Quarter, which is the largest unexplored desert in the world. This Hazarmaveth still holds its name, for Hadhramaut is only a modern rendering of Hazarmaveth.

As we trek eastward we come more and more "In the presence of Death", until at last we find in front of us a triangular oasis land with good water. At once the character of the land improves. Water is wealth to a desert land, and this Dhofar district is wealthy when compared with its neighbouring countries. The district of water-bearing country commences at Bander Reisut, an excellent anchorage for the gophers or for ships of the seagoing Ophir tribe.

They needed two anchorages, and Bander Reisut supplied the most important one for the initial stages of their seagoing development. Bander Reisut gave the anchorage for the strong Southern Monsoon, whilst Ras Merbat gave the northern anchorage for the Northern Monsoon, and half-way between these two harbours, right under the shadow of the purple-crowned hill Mount Sephar, there lay their *mesha*, or small trading port. This word *mesha* is often repeated in Arabian geography. Mocha, the port famous for its coffee, is a good example, but perhaps Mecca, the famous Holy City, is the best-known example of a *mesha* or trading centre. Later this *mesha* of the Ophir Land became the famous City of Ophir, and its ruins are still called "The City". Theodore Bent identifies it as the *mesha*

AT BEHAIR

THE TEMPLE GATE, OPHIR

THE LAND OF OPHIR

or trading place and Glaser identifies it as Ophir. The presence of these ruins proves the tribal location, and their position shows that it was the *mesha* of the Land of Ophir. I shall next turn to its later history and show that it developed from a *mesha* into the famous City of Ophir.

CHAPTER VIII

SULEIMAN

THE Queen of Sheba visited Suleiman and brought with her many gifts that were the trading samples of her lands. As a consequence a navy of Tharshish and a navy of Hiram, a vassal king, came to Suleiman's ports once every three years, bringing gold, silver, ivory, apes and peacocks.

Many investigators have attempted to locate Ophir, but at the time of their investigations there was no information regarding the gold of Arabia, and therefore they could not develop the Genesis information to advantage, and had to concentrate on the information regarding the cruise of Hiram. Here, again, they were handicapped, for, thinking the gold must necessarily be outside Arabia, they were inclined to place Ophir, the main Sabbaean port, far outside the Kingdom of Sabbaea. A three-year cruise seemed to give them great latitude in their researches, for a sailing ship can sail all round the world in three years. Magellan, the first of modern navigators to circumnavigate the globe, accomplished that feat in three years almost to the day; consequently the three-year cruise of

SULEIMAN

Hiram seemed to offer any locality for the location of Ophir.

For such theories they had to postulate that Ophir was a depot from which all the trading goods were brought, a somewhat impracticable suggestion; and further, they had to change the peacock to suit the locality which they located as Ophir. Their peacock, in fact, became an adaptable fowl, which was changed into anything short of the phœnix; the precise trading information was neglected, the greatest port of the Sabbaeans was often located far from the home of the Queen of Sheba, and the information which is actually so precise became absolutely indefinite.

Archæologists began to believe that there is insufficient information for the precise location of Ophir. Other critics studied the reign of Suleiman and came to the conclusion that his wealth and power were greatly exaggerated, and to them Ophir and the Ophir cruise began to look mythical. Western writers could gain little information about the Queen of Sheba. The cumulative effect of these investigations and their barren results gave the impression that the story of the Queen of Sheba and her port of Ophir were part of a romance designed to bring into prominence a ruler who was little more than a sheikh of bedou tribes who came to fleeting prosperity.

Only if we can bring sufficient evidence forward can we accept the story of Bilkis and Suleiman as being true; if we cannot, then we, too, should have to regard

TREASURE OF OPHIR

it merely as an Eastern romance glorifying a minor king and a mythical queen. In order the better to make our points we must examine the Biblical record of a trading cruise on a practical trading basis, using a knowledge of the sea and of ships. By employing practical trading principles we shall avoid the mistake of diverting a fleet from its proper trading grounds, and by following the cruise over its trading track we shall come to Ophir in due course.

From the Holy Q'ran we find that the name of the Queen of Sheba was Bilkis. When she went from Palestine to Abyssinia the people there called her Makeda—"It is not so"—and the Kebra Negast, the Abyssinian Bible, gives a great deal of information regarding her life in that country. From Arab histories and from the Kebra Negast we glean details of the life of this Eastern Queen from her childhood onward. I am compiling these notes at Azal, one of the capital towns of Sabbae, and a very prosperous city in the days when Bilkis the Beautiful was Queen of Sheba. The water-wheels creak all day, the sun burns down from a vivid blue sky and scorches the uncultivated land; the tilled land yields a harvest which is magnificent; the little asfari, the song-bird of Yemen, pours out his notes of liquid sweetness. Life is simple, needs are few. Such is the Land of Bilkis.

A mile and a half to the east is the mosque of Omdan. It is built on the foundations of the Omdan Palace, which the architects of Suleiman built for Bilkis,

SULEIMAN

and in the foundation of the mosque there is a carven stone which was one of the original stones of the Omdan Palace. Almost within sight of my house there is an ancient gold-mine which was worked in the days of Bilkis.

Whilst writing my notes I have ample time to study the history of Suleiman, and with Semitic speech in my ears I cannot bring myself to adopt the more general Greek spelling, "Solomon".

My library here is a small one, so I am not able fully to consult modern criticisms. Most of those I have consulted seem rather ignorant and stupid to me who am living in this land, where manners, customs and laws have remained unchanged for three thousand years. From one modern history I read that Suleiman was not a man of wondrous wisdom, but rather the cruel king of a savage people, who, by forced labour and reckless extravagance, won prosperity for a few years and then brought his tiny kingdom to inevitable ruin. As for Bilkis, the Great Queen of the South, apparently the historian does not even know her name. The Queen of Sheba is to him a myth woven into a tale of Eastern poetry.

If this is all that book-learning can do, I feel sorry for the Western savant. Let him scan instead the rolling seas, the trade winds, the changing monsoons, carven stones, broken idols, dusty relics, worn paths, little-known lands, and, above all, the loneliness and silence of the desert. All these have helped me in my search, so

TREASURE OF OPHIR

that here in the land where it was written, the history of Bilkis and Suleiman lives for me as a romance that shall never die, though it has lain buried in the dust of ages for three thousand years.

I peep through my window, and there, entering the city gateway, is a Sabbaean merchant strolling by in leisurely fashion. A gay silk turban crowns his head and he wears flowing robes with a long blue silk overcoat. About his waist he wears a belt of gold and silver brocade, studded with the agates of Beled er Rooss. In front of this belt he wears a dagger with a sheath of gold, and his sandals are richly embroidered with silver and silks. In him lives again Tamrin, that same merchant prince who helped Bilkis to weave the political schemes which should have united two Empires, but which were wrecked by a broken promise.

Tamrin passes through the city gate, and now there is a swirl of dust approaching from the northern road. A horseman comes into view, riding at full gallop his wild Arab steed, its nostrils aflare. It is Hudhud, the Ambassador of Suleiman. He, too, has ridden through three thousand years and is unchanged. In his turban there rests a small cylinder, the letter-satchel of the East. He bears with him the declaration of war which Bilkis changed to a message of peace. Take a glance at him, for he is a typical bedou sheikh, lean and brown, more at home in the saddle than in the house, and the look in his eyes speaks of wide horizons and desert sands.

SULEIMAN

Riding down the road on a hardy little donkey comes an Arab gentleman with a large leather-bound manuscript under his arm, making his way to my house. This is no fancy, for it is my friend Sheikh Omar, the Court Historian, carrying an ancient volume borrowed from the Imam's library. Unfortunately the title-page is missing, so I must collect my details from an unknown source, though I strongly suspect it may be a volume of Al Iklil, the treasured history of Arabia, written by Al Hamdani in the third year of Anno Hejira, nigh 1,350 years ago.

Living and working among these people, the story of Bilkis, read in her own lands, seems more alive than any Western romance. Suleiman came to the throne when a boy, and was seemingly the petty chieftain of a restless people. His father, David, was an old man, worn out by the strain and hardships of earlier campaigns. Adonijah, David's eldest surviving son, had attempted to usurp his father's throne, for in the Middle East of that time customs of heredity were the same as they are in Arabia to-day. The eldest son is not necessarily the heir. The king, if he is foreseeing and provident, calls a council, at which the right of succession is discussed. The eldest son has a strong hereditary claim, but popularity and ability are even more important factors.

After discussion the father nominates his successor, and that nomination is likely to stand, because his vote is usually decisive.

TREASURE OF OPHIR

David nominated Suleiman, the son of Bathsheba, who had been the widow of Uriah. It is not clear that David publicly nominated Suleiman, but he had given his promise to Bathsheba and the matter was known to his court. Directly Bathsheba informed David of the usurpation of Adonijah, David officially proclaimed Suleiman king, and he himself abdicated. Suleiman put down the rising without bloodshed and with a clemency that was extraordinary for the times in which he lived and which shows up very favourably in comparison with any incident of a similar type in European history.

His brother fled to sanctuary, and when he was arrested and brought before Suleiman he was merely sent to his own house under arrest. That was the judgment of Suleiman, a boy of fourteen at the time. David warned Suleiman that he must take stern measures with other dangerous persons in the kingdom. There was Joab, that cowardly and treacherous murderer of Amasa. Joab had also killed Absolam, when the latter was defenceless and entangled in a tree. It is doubtful whether David ever heard of those revolting details, but he recognized Joab as a particularly dangerous old man. Then there was Shimei, a loathsome character and a shifty intriguer. These were the two men whom David advised his son Suleiman to be rid of as soon as death had freed him of his father's obligations. There were other men also who were obviously dangerous and disloyal. Yet this young

SULEIMAN

ruler steered his country to prosperity through all this intrigue and with only three executions.

Within one year, and probably directly after David's death, Adonijah was again plotting dangerous intrigue. On that occasion the Princess Abishag, the priest Abiathar, Joab and Shimei were all implicated. By Suleiman's orders Adonijah and Joab (twice a murderer) were put to death. Joab had fled to sanctuary, but Suleiman refused him grace on account of his earlier record. Abiathar was banished to his own country, whilst Shimei was directed to build his house in Jerusalem and to remain there. He was also clearly warned that if he broke his parole he would be put to death, and Shimei acknowledged the justice of the sentence. Nothing was done to the Princess Abishag.

Again one is impressed with the extraordinary clemency with which Suleiman quashed an intrigue which was evidently a dangerous one. Later Shimei broke his parole, was caught, tried and executed. Those three executions are the sum total of deaths inflicted by Suleiman during a forty-years reign over a people who had proved themselves a restless and savage race. In the next reign they were again to prove themselves a quarrelsome collection of tribes, ready to throw away all those advantages of civilization which three successive rulers had gained for them in the short space of 120 years. Yet Suleiman has been described as a bloody ruler, when in fact he gave his lands unexampled peace and prosperity for forty years, at the cost of three worthless lives in the first four years of his reign.

His people could not be described as a nation, for they had not gained the unity of nationality. They had, however, a common aim which was akin to a national aim. By the development of that aim Suleiman led them to prosperity and founded a nation so strong that though, in later years, they were to meet with unparalleled misfortune, and have since that time been subjugated and dispossessed of their lands for thousands of years, they have always held, and they do still hold, a national sentiment stronger than any nation of any land in the world. If that were Suleiman's only achievement he would have won from history the right to be known as Suleiman the Wise.

In principle, the Jews and the Israelites held to monotheism, but in practice and prior to the days of Suleiman they had frequently turned aside to idol-worship and to polytheism. David had encouraged their ambitions and had accumulated large treasures for the building of a temple to their god Jehovah. Suleiman, at the age of eighteen, handled this problem with such skill that he won his people to a permanent monotheism, his country to a superb prosperity, and his lands to the position of the manufacturing centre of the civilized world.

Suleiman has been accused of a reckless extravagance that brought his kingdom to inevitable ruin. Let us turn for a minute to examine that accusation, for we

SULEIMAN

can do so with a minuteness that is surprising after a lapse of three thousand years. We know that the silver talent was worth four hundred pounds sterling. The gold talent was of different weight and is valued at two hundred and forty pounds sterling. With those estimates we can learn that an Egyptian horse brought to Palestine was worth an average of seventeen pounds ten shillings, and an Egyptian chariot was delivered in Palestine at seventy pounds. That suggests silver and gold had a purchasing power approximating to silver and gold at the sterling rate of the present day. Consequently we can estimate fairly closely the value of the gold and silver treasure stored by King David, but as for the other accumulated treasures we can only make rough estimates.

David told Suleiman that he had stored 100,000 talents of gold and 1,000,000 talents of silver. The sterling value of that treasure works out at four hundred and twenty-four million pounds sterling. Considering the fact that all loot for thirty years and more had been added to the revenue, this estimate is not beyond probability. A further voluntary subscription of five million two hundred thousand pounds was added, making a total capital of over four hundred and twenty-nine million pounds, and in addition to this there was a vast store of jewellery, precious stones, other metals, hewn stone, seasoned wood and temple furniture.

If we can regard David's statement as an accurate one, then Suleiman apparently possessed a capital of well over five hundred million pounds in metal and material for the building of the Temple and palace. It may be that David was speaking in round numbers only and was using the figurative method of speech which is so common to Orientals, but even so, it is difficult to imagine that the Temple and palace cost more than ten million pounds sterling, when so much building material and precious stones were already in hand, and moreover, it is certain that Suleiman commenced his work with a capital far in excess of that ten million pounds. We are quite sure of this when we realize that more than five million pounds was raised by one voluntary subscription, and that added to this was the accumulation of revenue and the loot from more than thirty years of successful warfare.

When we remember too, the vast amount of precious metal and the material at Suleiman's disposal, yet another criticism vanishes. It is a very foolish criticism, but it has been so often repeated that it needs to be dispelled. Commentators frequently point out that Suleiman built a far larger house for himself than he did for Jehovah. But the Temple of Jehovah was an architectural jewel which did not need to be large, for it was not a place of worship like the church or cathedral of temperate climates. The Temple was simply the House of God, with its inner sanctuary and its outer house, from whence the priests issued to an open-air service held before a congregation assembled in the outer porches. On occasions when the oracles

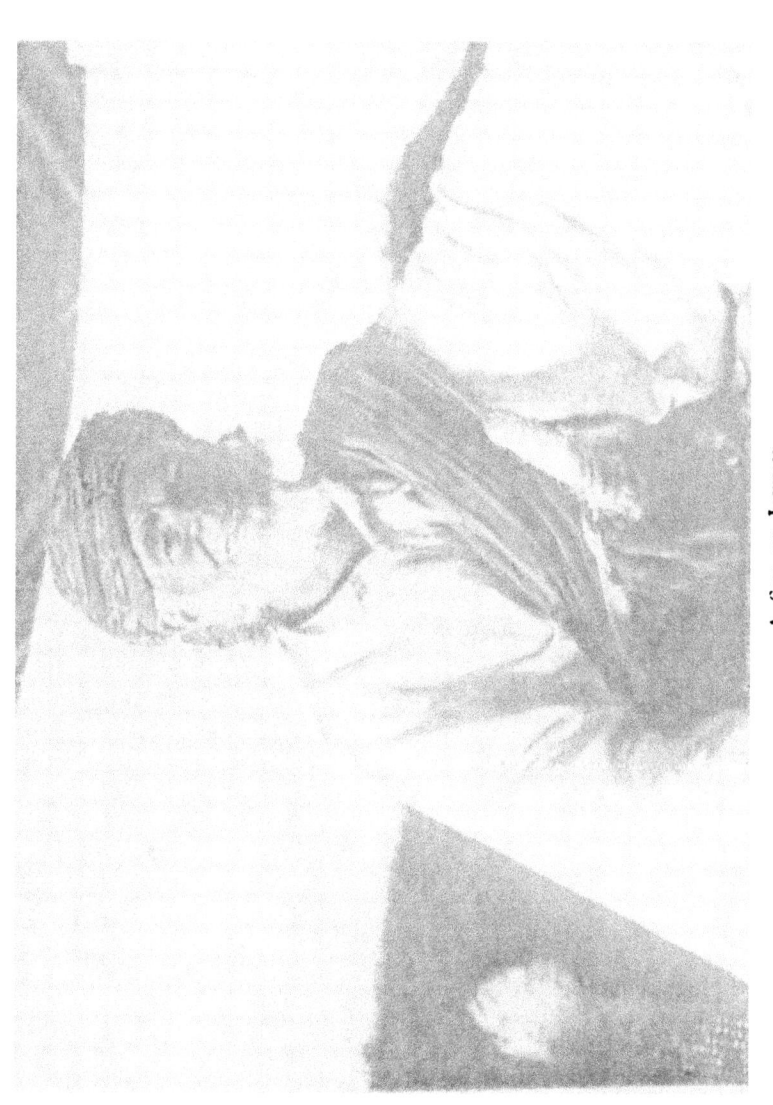

A Son of Joktan

[Facing page 216

SULEIMAN

were consulted it is possible that royalty and sheikhs of the ruling order were admitted, for they were Defenders of the Faith, but even that suggestion is doubtful.

On the other hand, the House of Solomon, the House of Lebanon, and the Queen's palace were State buildings and necessarily large. They were not merely private houses, they were needed for the vast hospitalities of the richest State in the Middle East. Those royal palaces were very well built, but when we examine the enthusiastic accounts of them they do not appear to have been ornamented with disproportionate extravagance. It does appear that after completing the Temple, the palace and the porches, there was still a large surplus of gold. That surplus was reduced by a further furnishing of the House of Lebanon, but, considering the large capital at his disposal, Suleiman had no serious financial worry. He had, however, serious political difficulties to face.

To north of him lay the great Assyrian Empire, ready to advance so soon as the northern borders of Suleiman's mushroom kingdom showed signs of weakness. Suleiman had reason to fear Assyrian intrigue and Assyrian hostility, but by maintaining his building activities he could keep the northern regions in employment, and consequently prosperous and contented.

To the south there lay the ancient Egyptian Empire, and, although he was married to Pharaoh's daughter, he well knew that the political support he enjoyed was a somewhat feeble prop and certainly would not outlast his own lifetime. Meanwhile he was encouraging trade with Egypt.

His people had learnt the art of dyeing and of spinning whilst making the priestly vestments of the Temple, and in this connection we must bear in mind that only the best workmanship was accepted for the Temple and the Temple furniture. When we read of the vast amount of Temple furniture and vestments it becomes clear that each branch founded an industry that was new to a people who were only freshly emerging from a bedou, or at the best a pastoral stage.

Money had not yet reached the coinage stage. Large sums were paid in ingots, such as the silver talent of over 117lbs. troy, the gold talent which was worth fifteen silver shekels, and the gold shekel which weighed two hundred and fifty-three grains. There were also fractions of a shekel, but there is no evidence that actual coins had yet come into being. One must suppose that an economic genius such as Suleiman fully realized the handicap of a somewhat clumsy system of barter. To have instituted coinage Suleiman would have needed to institute a Royal Mint and a Royal Treasury, but a law contained in an ancient prophecy debarred him from accumulating a Royal Treasury unless it was clearly designed for a religious purpose, such as that accumulated by King David. Now that the Temple was built he had no excuse for accumulating further stores of money and jewels.

By the manufacture of large quantities of Temple

SULEIMAN

furniture, however, Suleiman succeeded in encouraging labour, and also kept the State finances in a fluid condition in a manner that had never been approached by other monarchs. Thus, although he could not accumulate treasure, or, as we should say, "could not bank his revenue", he invested it in the best possible way. Even in these days we consider building is a good form of investment, and Suleiman not only built costly palaces, but he also built many cities and kept the frontier cities well fortified.

CHAPTER IX

SULEIMAN—*continued*

THE Hebrew records, anxious to laud the power of this great ruler, give the impression that Suleiman expanded his kingdom enormously, and over-expansion has often been suggested as the main cause of the rapid decline and fall of the Kingdom of Suleiman. When we examine these Hebrew records, we find that there were no wars of expansion. King David had expanded the kingdom till its borders reached Mesopotamia to the north, and Egypt to the south. Suleiman, by wise policies, strengthened that kingdom, but did not commit the mistake of former Middle Eastern rulers.

He strengthened his kingdom to such an extent that the rulers of neighbouring lands paid him tribute as a matter of policy, but not owing to the military occupation of their land by his armies. At the same time Suleiman did not ignore military requirements. He expanded his standing army from 1,400 chariots to 4,000 chariots, which were well-stabled, and mainly stationed in the border cities. His cavalry he increased from 1,200 horsemen to 12,000 horsemen. That standing army was entirely recruited from his own people,

SULEIMAN

and did not include any mercenaries. His own people were tax free, and were not subjected to forced labour. The foreigners in his land were subjected to a tax of one-third of their time, devoted to State labour. It is interesting to bear those facts in mind, for later, when Jeroboam headed a protest and revolt, we see that his complaint against forced labour was a political move, rather than the voicing of a genuine grievance.

If we require further evidence as to the state of Suleiman's kingdom, we get it both from Tamrin, a Sabbaean merchant, who visited Jerusalem about this time, and also from Bilkis, the kindly Queen of a prosperous country. The evidence of Tamrin is particularly valuable, for he gave witness in his own country, and at a time when the Sabbaean Court were in a mood hostile to Suleiman. In each case the evidence is the same. Both Bilkis and Tamrin were emphatic in their praise, both of Suleiman and his administration. They both expressed the opinion that the subjects of Suleiman were particularly happy and fortunate. It is only fair to add that Bilkis gave this evidence *before* she married the king.

In increasing his standing army Suleiman was again handicapped by the law contained in the old prophecy which we have already mentioned. He was not able to send his own people to Egypt to purchase horses or chariots, the main requirements of his standing army. He had to purchase these requirements through the medium of former adversaries, the Syrians and Hittites.

TREASURE OF OPHIR

Working on a bold and grand scale, he overcame the main difficulty by horse-breeding in his own lands. In ten years of reign he had brought his kingdom to an extraordinary state of prosperity, yet he was very near to failure.

He had been married as a child of twelve, and now he had a son named Rehoboam eleven years old. Suleiman knew that his son would not be able to hold his people with a firm hand. Apart from such character as the boy had developed, he would have a politico-religious handicap which would rob him of the support which he would most require. In the Middle East of to-day we can clearly see the handicap that proved fatal to that boy. Semitic peoples of the Middle East, Jews, Israelites, and Arabs, have always regarded religion as the source of all wisdom. Therefore they always attempt to give a religious aspect to whatever policies they adopt.

Religious motive may be fanned to fanaticism, consequently Semitic policies of the Middle East may be subject to violent upheavals. Every ruler must encounter opposition, and Suleiman well knew that the opposition to Rehoboam would prove beyond control. The boy's mother was Naamah, an Ammonite woman, and probably an Ammonite princess.

The Ammonites were hereditary enemies of the Beni Israel, and moreover, they were not worshippers of Jehovah. How could the son of a heathen woman become the religious leader of a restless people, whose

SULEIMAN

strongest motives to unity was a particular monotheism? If he were the only son of Suleiman he would succeed to the throne, but he had little chance of holding his people in political unity.

Suleiman reached the zenith of his prosperity about the tenth year of his reign, the 414th year after the Exodus. In the tenth year, and about the month of Abid, which corresponds to April, some six months before the opening of the Temple, Suleiman was only twenty-five, and he might hope for another son, who would succeed to the throne without such heavy handicaps. That was only one of Suleiman's anxieties, serious enough to a man who had been married twelve years.

His more serious problem was one that has faced many a Middle Eastern ruler, and has wrecked many a promise of prosperity. Within the next decade, Palestine, and the Protectors of Palestine, are likely to face this same problem, which is that of the bedou, those homeless sons of Ishmael, whose instincts and training are wedded to ambitions of plunder. Once aroused, their hostility is implacable. They are weak, but they are persistent. A swift raid, a little plunder; then again a little raid, with a few sheep, goats, and camels for loot. Those are the bedou methods. No single raid is very serious, yet the cumulative effect is disastrous. The borders are disturbed, the unrest grows, the trade routes are cut. Reprisals take place, but the unrest is interminable. Added to those evils the bedou exhibit a genius for petty intrigue; eventually their destructive activities drain the resources of a kingdom. One can hardly call their intrigues policies; they are too shiftless for that.

Throughout history those Ishmaelities have hardly shown any power to construct, only to destroy, though at first sight the Moslem Empire of the Omayides and Abassides suggests that the Ishmaelites are capable of constructive policies. Fired with the pure religious zeal of Monotheism, the Muslim swept all-conquering through the Middle East and into Western Europe. Soon, perhaps too soon, their religious zeal evaporated, or was tainted by luxury. Then the force of civilization swept the Ishmaelites back to their own lands. There they dwelt to reflect that their prophet preached the religion of Islam "Peace", and not the religion of the sword.

With those ideals no longer tainted, but refined by misfortune, they are spreading their faith through darkest Africa, and through many a land that has not yet learned the power of Monotheism. So long as the Moslem holds to the ideals of his Faith, he will be a blessing and a good influence to the world. But so long as the Ishmaelite holds to his senseless greed and desire for loot and plunder, he will remain a pariah of civilization.

Suleiman, with political genius, saw the only solution to the bedou problem. It is the solution that is open to the Palestine of the present day. The bedou

SULEIMAN

cannot be pacified by direct trade. He has his tiny exports, but he needs no imports other than gold, with which he purchases military power and buys trouble for his neighbour; but he can be quietened by indirect trade methods.

East of Palestine lay the bedou of Ishmaelite strain, but farther east again the Kahtanis, the industrious Arabs, who were ruled by Queen Bilkis. Her empire at that time was an old and well-established one, and that kingdom held the far-famed port of Ophir, the most flourishing seaport of its time, and the most famous trading port of the world. If Suleiman could establish political connection and trading activity with Ophir and the Land of Ophir, then the Ishmaelite lands would become the ferry-ground between the Ophir Lands, that are also called the Sabbaean Empire, and Palestine, the Kingdom of Suleiman. The need was with Suleiman; the choice was with Bilkis. Her kingdom traded with India, China, Persia, and Africa.

Ophir had traded with the West, and did carry on a small trade with Egypt and with Palestine, but its main trade was with the Eastern lands, and it was doubtful whether Sabbaea would reap any sufficient economic advantages by extending her trade and commitments to Western spheres. Suleiman had attempted to get into political communication with Bilkis, and up to the present he had met with no success. He had sent his ambassador to her, and, in return, Tamrin, the Sabbaean merchant prince, had paid a visit to the

TREASURE OF OPHIR

Court of Suleiman. Beyond a polite return visit to Tamrin, negotiations had proceeded no further. Now Suleiman had sent another envoy, and was awaiting his return. If the reply were unfavourable, then Suleiman saw no alternative but to gain by force what was denied to diplomacy. He realized that with the bedou problem unsolved, his kingdom was doomed to a short existence. It would be better to force the issue whilst he was at the summit of his power, instead of awaiting a less favourable opportunity.

At the same time he fully realized the difficulty of such a course. If he declared war on Sabbaea his army would first have to traverse some 1,000 miles of country which is mainly inhospitable. Then, with his lines of communication stretched to this great distance, his army would be faced with a chain of mountains which rise from the Tihima sea-level to 7,000 and 9,000 feet. Throughout history that barrier has proved impregnable. The only invader who appears to have made any appreciable warlike incursion into that country was Zeizan, the king of Yemen, who was driven from his lands, and fled to Persia. He persuaded his Persian protector to fit out an expedition for him, and landed at Aden, after losing some of his troops by shipwreck. His successes from Aden to Sanaa appear to have been mainly diplomatic ones, and in all probability he encountered no serious opposition.

Suleiman had no such easy alternative open to him. Probably at this time he had no ships at all, or possibly

SULEIMAN

a small navy manned by Hiram's people, but certainly not by his own. His own people were not sea-going, and never had been. True, he had the small tribe of Danites on the Mediterranean coasts, but they were not true Beni Israel, and had only lately come under his sway. It was impractical for him to consider any invasion by sea; he would have to invade Sabbaea through Assir (the Difficult Land), or through other mountain ranges equally difficult.

A successful war on Sabbaea might be possible, since he had a genius for political work, and would get tribes to join his forces as they advanced southwards; but he would be undertaking an expedition that had never been successful in history, and which, incidentally, has proved too difficult for any military leader up to the present time. On the other hand, if he did not succeed in establishing his influence in Sabbaea, his kingdom would be weakened, drained, and disrupted by the bedou of his Eastern borders.

CHAPTER X

THE QUEEN OF SHEBA

BILKIS, the Queen of Sheba, is the national heroine of Yemen, the land of her birth. There is, of course, a certain amount of exaggeration in the Arab history which deals with Bilkis and her time, for it was the Golden Age of Southern Arabia. It seems that Sabbaea owed its prosperity mainly to the Ophir tribes, who had founded their *mesha* in the early post-diluvian days, and had developed the trading port until it became the world-famed City of Ophir, with two subsidiary ports, Bander Reisut and Ras Merbat.

The ante-diluvians had been able to build great ships. Their Ophir descendants had access to those earlier records which were, of course, handed down with the Flood records; but they would not have needed sea-going ships until their own drowned lands were sufficiently developed to require overseas trade. At least 500 years before Suleiman and Bilkis, the oversea trade of Ophir was developing. At about 1500 B.C. the Sabbaeans built the great dam of Mareb. That shows that they were then a cultured race, with great engineers, and therefore we may presume they had other

THE QUEEN OF SHEBA

abilities fully developed. They enclosed the outlet between two hill ranges, and thereby formed a great lake.

Mareb is at a height of some 7,000 feet above sea level, and catches the rainfall of both the north and south monsoon. Intervening there are months of drought, when the hot Arabian sun scorches the land, during December, January, and part of February, and again during part of April and May. The land is mainly of volcanic origin, so the soil is not very retentive, and well-water runs deep, but with the great dam of Mareb there was sufficient water reserve to tide over the months of drought, and give prosperity to all the surrounding country.

On my journeys through Yemen I have frequently found water-cisterns and large tanks, some of which are vaguely classified as Himmiarrite in origin, whilst others are said to be Roman. The Romans did garrison Yemen for a time, and were eventually absorbed by the Southern Arabs, who can be classified as either Himmiarrites or Homerites. It is unlikely that the Romans were in ascendancy sufficiently long to do more than repair already existing systems of water conduit. Apparently in the 1500 B.C. era the Southern Arabs had developed a water system that made use of mountain gorges, and tanks which were used as water reservoirs.

The Tuweila Tanks at Aden may well be a last link in a chain of one of these systems. The tanks of the present are only a part of the Sabbaean tanks, whose ruins were found in the Aden hills, yet they have a capacity far larger than is required for the normal rainfall of Aden. It is unlikely that engineers would have undertaken unnecessary work, whereas, if the Tuweila Tanks were part of a chain, then their connection with the Wadi Kebir of Lahej kept them filled all the year round, and they had an overflow outlet to the sea. The Sabbaeans probably developed their system with these reservoirs, till they kept a water flow from Wadi to Wadi, giving fertility from their heights right down to the sea-level. The reservoir system was only taxed for a maximum of a three-months' stretch. That was the position in the Sabbaean era of 1500 B.C. to about 500 B.C., an era which includes the time of Bilkis and Suleiman.

Then comes the Himmiarrite era. The change in name is not owing to invasion, as Western historians have suggested. Himyar was a patriarch of the Southern Arabs, and for several centuries the Sabbaeans followed the cult of Himyar, which was later replaced by the cult of Omar, from whence we gain the name Homerites. Geographical conditions have rendered Southern Arabia immune from invasion: to this day the laws and customs of Yemen are the same as they were in the days of Bilkis 1000 B.C., and are said to be the same as they were 1,000 years earlier than Bilkis.

Bilkis passed her childhood in Abyssinia. When we look at a map we are apt to regard Abyssinia and

CARVEN STONES NEAR SANAA

THE QUEEN OF SHEBA

Northern Africa as definitely separated from Southern Arabia. In English history Great Britain has kept in close connection with France, yet France and Britain are more definitely separated by geographical conditions than Southern Arabia and Abyssinia. Arabs cross to Abyssinia by canoe every day of the week, passing through the Gate of Tears, which is better known as Bab el Mandeb, or the Straits of Perim.

In Genesis days the Cushites, sons of Ham, first colonized Southern Arabia, and then crossed over to Abyssinia. Semitic tribes who were mainly Joktani, sons of Joktan, then dispossessed the Cushites of Southern Arabia. In 1000 B.C. we find the Joktani Sabbaeans in full possession of Southern Arabia and Abyssinia. Sabbaea is the land of Sheba, and Sheba means either "seven" or "agate". We do not definitely know the names of the seven provinces to which Bilkis, Queen of Sheba, succeeded, but it is certain that the part of her kingdom which later became Yemen is a land where agate is plentiful.

Starting life in Abyssinia, and in the province of Axum, she was captured by a savage tribe of the forests and was bound to a tree, as propitiation to the forest god, which was probably a leopard. She was rescued, and apparently only in the nick of time, for the muscles of her foot were torn, and she was rendered lame for all her youth. When she met Suleiman, a happy accident freed these damaged muscles, and this was regarded as a miracle performed

TREASURE OF OPHIR

by Suleiman. The Kebra Negast gives many details of this story, but veils most of it in legend.

We can reconstruct some of the details of the accession of Bilkis, for the same accession customs are operative in Yemen to this day. The ruler is elected, and does not succeed by hereditary right. There is a general election by the showing of hands, women having equal voting rights with men. The candidates are grouped according to political classification, and when only one group remains then individual selection commences. In practice there are no freak elections, for the selection is always made from amongst the members of the ruling family, who are well-known to the people. When the individual is elected as ruler, his election is for life duration.

It seems that Bilkis met a certain amount of unrest at the commencement of her reign, and she put down all insurrection with such severity that she earned the reputation of being a she-devil. As she grew up she developed an excessive growth of hair on her legs, and by the time she visited Suleiman rumours were current that she was a devil with goat's feet! A young girl, lame, of strong character, and with a growth of hair on her legs! These three characteristics were sufficient for the formation of many legends regarding the Queen of Sheba and her malignant powers. From Abyssinian folk-lore, and mainly from the Kebra Negast, the Abyssinian Bible, we can gain many details if we can rightly separate fact from fiction.

THE QUEEN OF SHEBA

From Arab histories we glean further facts about Bilkis, but here again we meet with poetic exaggeration. At Mareb her palace held one thousand people; it had pillars of white wood, each pillar being 100 cubits high. Her army had one thousand officers, each in command of one thousand men. Sometimes these statements of the strength of her forces are multiplied by ten. From this mass of evidence we have to select probabilities, but it is very likely we at times under-estimate facts, for at present it is difficult to realize the prosperity that must have existed throughout Sabbaea, and which could be revived in the present generation. For my facts I have relied mainly on the Arab manuscripts, unearthed by the Court Historian of the Imam of Yemen.

He used to call on me and boast in vague terms about the beauty of Bilkis and the glories of Sabbaea, but when I asked for details he preferred keeping to generalities, and would tell me at length of Saif Zeizan, another hero of Yemen. I heard plenty about Saif Zeizan, his mountains of gold, his generosity when a prisoner, his personal bravery, and so on, but he did not belong to the Bilkis period, and I had no interest in him. "Sheikh Omar," I said, "I will tell you more about Bilkis than you know." At this the most learned historian of Yemen was roused to defend his reputation. "She was short, dark, and rather fat," I suggested, and hinted that I could find those details and others written in European books. Omar was indignant. He searched the Imam's library, and from the

TREASURE OF OPHIR

mosque of Omdan brought the precious manuscripts from which I have gleaned so much. Local knowledge and assistance from sheiks of other Yemen cities built up a story so instinct with life that I was sorely tempted to clothe the dry bones of history with the soft draperies of romance. I have overcome that temptation, but hope that before very long some skilled author will undertake this task.

It seems that Suleiman had been carrying forward protracted negotiations with Bilkis; probably he desired to get into trading relations with Sabbaea as soon as his Temple building was commenced, for he needed the Gold of Ophir, the precious stones of Sabbaea, the Almug trees, which were only obtainable from Ophir districts, and, of course, he required the very best incense, the famous spices of Hazarmaveth. Up to the present he had failed to get into close touch with the Queen of Sheba, and now, therefore, he sent Hudhud, his ambassador, with a final message.

She was by this time well established as Queen of the Sabbaean Empire, and she held autocratic rule over all Arabia proper, and over Abyssinia. Her Sabbaean outposts were widely scattered through the Far East, and the Himmiarrite ruins of those outposts have led to suggestions that Ophir may have been situated far from Southern Arabia. Himmiarritic ruins do no more than indicate the seafaring activities of the Sabbaeans, and not necessarily even that. Oval-shaped walls may show the temple of a sun-worshipping people,

THE QUEEN OF SHEBA

and a strong wall surrounding the temple may be typically Sabbaean, but these do not signify that the race came from Sabbaea.

The oval-shaped wall is almost certainly the indication of a race which studied astronomy, and probably of a race of sun-worshippers. We know that the Adamite races were widely dispersed, and that suggests that the cult of the sun and the cult of astronomy was widespread, but astronomical indications do little to help us in tracing the Sabbaeans. We must expect to find the main port of the Sabbaeans in Sabbaea itself, and the surest means of tracing the outposts of Sabbaea are by studying the activities of her people and noting where those activities led them.

Tribal information, and the mention of *mesha*, places the Ophir tribe definitely on the Southern Arabian sea-coast. The words Ophir and Gopher seem closely connected, and that is a useful hint. A coastal tribe whose shores were open to the steady breezes of the north and south monsoons, must necessarily have developed into a seagoing tribe. Having good harbours along their coasts, they naturally developed the best harbour as their main seaport, and from thence they traded wherever the monsoon winds blew them. With the support of the Sabbaean ruins, and with the evidence of the trade winds, we find Sabbaean outposts at Kishm in the Persian Gulf, Karachi on the north-west coast of India, Ceylon off Southern India, and Calcutta on the north-east coast. Moreover, all the Somali coasts give us plenty of evidence of Sabbaean activities, and the Sabbaean ruins of Zimbabwe take us right down the east coast of Africa to the ancient post of Sofala. Chinese evidence suggests that they traded also with the Far East. Having once become a sea-going tribe—and that was long before the days of Bilkis, and continued long after that date—there was nothing to stop the Sabbaeans from trading and cruising all round the world.

At the time of Bilkis the Sabbaean Empire consisted of Northern Arabia and Abyssinia, with the empire capital at Mareb, the main seaport at Ophir. Northern Arabia came under Sabbaea, but had a more colonial type of rule, and there were also the trading outposts of Kism, Colombo, Calcutta, and East African ports, roughly as far south as Dar es Salaam. At Mareb her palace was called Dar s Saleh, "The House of Happiness".

Writing these notes at Sanaa, some fifty miles west of Mareb, I can amplify bare historical statements with local information, and can tint the scenes with local colour.

When describing Dar s Saleh, the palace of Bilkis, the Arab historians have exaggerated its magnificence beyond reasonable possibility. They do, however, give sufficient information for us to get a fairly accurate picture of this ancient palace. The Arab Red City, the Alhambra of Granada, Spain, gives us a good example of some of the leading features. The Alhambra was more artistic, but not so magnificent, nor so large as the

THE QUEEN OF SHEBA

Dar s Saleh. The Dar s Saleh, of course, overlooked Moeris, the royal lake of Mareb, which was formed by the Dam of Mareb. The Arab has always understood the value of a water-front, and of courtyards with fountains near to his dwelling. The palace was built within a citadel that was also a garden city.

As I write these notes, I keep refreshing my memory by going to the house-top and noting the details of the Dar s Saleh of the Imam of Yemen, which occupies the western corner of the walled city of Sanaa. It is said that the Dar s Saleh of Bilkis was built for ten thousand people, but evidently what is meant is, that the Dar s Saleh walls embraced a citadel like the Alhambra, and in this citadel were ten thousand people, though I suspect the true number was one thousand, and the multiplication is Oriental exaggeration.

In the Garden of Happiness were Nim, Apricot, Fig, Peach, Walnut, Mahogany, Banyan, Pear, Almond, Acacia, Cedar and Palm trees. There were, of course, many other types of tree, but the most beautiful was the spreading palm, though the date palm does not show at its best in these highlands, for it is a tree of the Arabian lowlands. In the gardens they could grow many flowers, including sunflowers, marigold, and all the daisy tribe, with most of the European flowers that enjoy light soil.

Roses flourish very well in these highlands, but I do not suppose the gardens of the Dar s Saleh would compare well with European flower-gardens, for the

TREASURE OF OPHIR

Sabbaeans were singularly inartistic, and their Arab descendants pay little attention to flower cultivation, and even in vegetable-growing show a lack of knowledge which is distressing. Yemen soil can grow excellent vegetables, but the native prefers size to delicacy of flavour, whilst with his fruit he loses much of the delicate flavour by plucking it before it is fully ripened. Only in the grape is he a real connoisseur, and grows some twenty different species in his vineyards.

The palace itself was an impressive building of very heavy architecture, but its massiveness somewhat relieved by reason of its three storeys being built of different material. The ground floor was of hewn stone faced with lime cement, but the upper storeys were faced with gold and inlaid with the many-coloured agates and cornelians which are so plentiful in the Sabbaean lands, whilst the topmost storey was of red and white marble.

Over a flat roof was a crown of golden domes, which would serve as small cupolas for resting in during the cool hours of the day. The ground floor was faced with a veranda supported by pillars of Almug timber, a tall white tree very different from the Algum tree.

In the evening when the sun was setting behind the purple hills and the Lake Moeris turned to gold, the Dar s Saleh must have been a beautiful sight for the townsfolk of that ancient city Mareb, which is now a mass of ruins, guarded by bedou of the most primitive type.

THE QUEEN OF SHEBA

I have tried to go to Mareb and have interviewed many of the sheikhs of the district, but I learn that at present the expedition is hardly feasible. If I took with me a herd of cattle as a present to the Sheikh of Mareb then I might reach Mareb in safety, but it is very doubtful whether I should leave there without trouble.

I am advised to take with me an Arab wife, and leave her as a hostage when I returned to Sanaa and civilization. That method has been adopted with success by two Arab travellers who now live at Sanaa, and I pass on the hint since I do not intend to take advantage of it, and at present am content to study the descriptions found in Arab manuscripts.

According to these, the interior of the palace was very magnificent, for the ceilings were covered with polished red and rock crystals. In an Arab room the main feature is the daïs, which nowadays is well-carpeted with Persian rugs and furnished with small bolsters, stuffed with native cotton, and covered with silk or satin. This daïs is a part of the room and is some two and a half feet wide and raised eighteen inches above floor-level. In the throne-room of the Dar s Saleh the daïs was covered with gold and was studded with emeralds and rubies. The only Arab emeralds I have seen were of a very light colour, and the Arabian ruby was probably a poor-grade carborundum, but both stones can be obtained from Arabia. This throne became famous through history and was probably a very striking piece of furniture. It is said that all furniture

TREASURE OF OPHIR

was of gold, and if this refers merely to the coffee-tables the description is not an extravagant one.

The Arab keeps remarkably little movable furniture in his house. He uses piles of rugs and cushions on the floor, and needs no chairs or writing-tables. His walls are full of niches, in which are stowed all books and writing materials, and he hardly uses book-cases or cupboards. Practically the only portable furniture is a light metal table composed of two trays with a cylinder some twelve inches long between them. This makes a table sufficiently high for serving coffee, and as soon as one side is coffee-stained the servant turns the table upside down, thus presenting a clean tray.

Sitting in my Arab room with walls all ornamented and lighted with fretted windows of stained glass, I asked Sheikh Omar if he thought the Dar s Saleh was similarly ornamented and if he could find any reference to that point. He answered that it was highly unlikely that the Dar s Saleh had any such adornment, as the present design of Arab houses at Sanaa was brought from Palestine when the Queen of Sheba returned with architects of Suleiman. He said that the rooms of the Dar s Saleh probably had plain white walls, unrelieved by any ornamentation, and the rooms would be littered with trays, water-carafes and hand-basins all of gold. Next we turn our attention to the life led by Bilkis. Here we are very fortunate, for all my friends at Sanaa, from His Highness the Imam down, assured me that civilization had changed so little

SANAA FROM THE HOUSE-TOP
IMAM'S PALACE, CENTRE

THE QUEEN OF SHEBA

in Yemen since the days of Bilkis that we could regard the normal life of the present upper-class typical of her time, and moreover that the life of the present ruler would in no way differ from that of Queen Bilkis.

The ruler rises early, has a cup of kishr (aromatic tea, brewed from coffee husks), and, as coffee is indigenous to the land, it is probable that Queen Bilkis, too, had her cup of kishr and with it a small plate of milk-curds, for that also is a dish very popular throughout Arabia. In the fruit season there were also available figs, grapes, apricots, prickly pears, ordinary pears, pomegranates, and several kinds of melon, but the early morning meal is a very light one and scarcely corresponds to more than our morning tea and biscuits.

Bilkis, in the early days of her reign, was a sun-worshipper, and at sunrise she went to her temple for the morning service. On returning she held Court for a couple of hours, listening to plaints and petitions. This Court was held in public, and any subject had access to the Ruler, just as is the case in the present day. I have watched the Imam of Yemen, seated on a wooden chair, in a public thoroughfare, holding his morning Court, listening to small cases, such as those concerning trespass or the ownership of a calf that has been offered in pledge.

About 10 a.m. Bilkis would close her public Court and take the first real meal of the day, and, as the next meal was at sunset, both this breakfast and the evening meal were substantial.

TREASURE OF OPHIR

Afternoon tea or light refreshment is not a custom of Yemen, though in the fruit season a bunch of grapes is sometimes served in the afternoon. After breakfast Bilkis would open her Court to the ministers, and from then onwards there was little rest, for hospitality claimed the remainder of her day. About sunset she would take her evening ride, and during a busy period it is probable she would work late into the night. I have known many Arab rulers who work until midnight and then recommence their day before sunrise, but in such cases it is customary for them to take two or three hours' rest in the afternoon. This evening work provides a rather interesting spectacle. The gathering for the evening meal is a large one, for most of the ministers are present, and after the meal all adjourn to the living-room, where cushions are arranged around the walls. Little tables are then brought in, coffee is served, and finally a slave brings in a tray of correspondence, which is handed to the Ruler.

He peruses each letter, screws it up into a ball and tosses it over to the minister it concerns. Each recipient scribbles a note, and perhaps passes it over to another minister, so that by the end of the evening the floor is littered with rolls and balls of paper, which are later swept up and burnt. During the evening business session there is little conversation, although there is no rule about strict silence. At about 10 p.m. the town-guard gathers outside the palace and sings the National

THE QUEEN OF SHEBA

Anthem. I asked for the words, but the Town Governor, who was my host, replied that he doubted whether anyone really knew them. He himself had learned the Anthem in his childhood, and forgotten it later, but so long as everyone stuck to the tune the words did not matter. (Incidentally, I must say that I have noticed the same peculiarity with regard to the British National Anthem.) The Arabian tune is a lively hill-song which runs up and down the scale and finally reaches a crescendo shout. "How old is your Anthem?" I inquired. "Tell me, first, how old is Yemen?" laughed the Amil.

During my stay at Sanaa I wanted to learn something of the justice and of the legal administration of that land whose laws are said to have remained unchanged for thousands of years. I suggested that the laws could not be so ancient as is claimed. "But, my friend," answered the Wazir, or Imam's Prime Minister, "you forget that Mahomedt our Blessed Prophet founded his laws on those which already existed." I answered that the laws of the Holy Q'ran are based on the Mosaic Law, to which the Wazir retorted that the Mosaic Law was an adjustment of the laws of the bedou tribes, and these laws had emanated from Yemen, the most ancient of the settled lands of Arabia. He said that the laws were probably framed in Sareh-ail-al-Himmiarri, the ancient universal language of Arabia, and the name Sareh-ail-al-Himmiarri suggests that language was in use almost as early as the time of the patriarch Abraham, so that the laws possibly date back to that early age.

Capital punishment is seldom inflicted and there is very little imprisonment. The main prevention of crime lies in the prompt settlement of cases of public punishment. I did not consider it desirable or necessary to witness any of the public punishments, but from inquiries I gathered that it is severe but not cruel. During my eight months' stay at Sanaa there were only two serious crimes. An Army officer had committed a minor offence and a guard was sent to arrest him. In panic the officer started using his rifle. His house was stormed and he was shot dead, but he killed two people whilst resisting arrest.

The second crime was committed by three men who attempted to rob a mosque of some carpets. They were caught red-handed, arrested, and brought before the Imam. They were given full and careful trial, and encouraged to put forward their defence. Being judged guilty, they were chained to the city walls during the daylight hours of seven days, but the enchainment was not cruel and they were well guarded from molestation. They were publicly whipped on the first and last days of punishment, but this by no means resembled the cruel flogging of Western administration. They were whipped across the shoulders with a cane of moderate weight, and the striker administered the blows from the elbow, and not from his shoulder muscles.

I had the good fortune to test Yemen administration

THE QUEEN OF SHEBA

with a personal case, and also with a case in which my secretary was the plaintiff. The best evidence of my confidence of justice rests in the fact that in each affair I had ample opportunity of settling the matter out of Court.

I had a horse which was liable to kick, and when I bought it one of the Imam's grooms warned me, and I took full notice of the warning. My groom used to take the horse to water at a trough in the town; there was a drinking-trough in our garden, but he enjoyed a chat with his fellow-grooms and liked showing off the paces of the horse. One evening Yehia, the groom, returned with a confused story of how the horse had grown restive and had kicked a child, whose father now wanted compensation, alleging that the child had been hurt.

I was not satisfied with Yehia's explanations, but awaited developments, for I knew that if a child had been hurt my medicine-box would be called for. Later the father came round and suggested that I should pay compensation. Satisfied that no one had been hurt, I replied that the matter did not concern me, and any grievances must be settled with the groom, who was in charge of the horse. Later an Arab friend came and offered his good services as mediator. I replied that I knew there was something amiss and I should like to have the matter settled in Court, as I had no desire to lay myself open to blackmail.

The Cadi, or magistrate, called next day and

suggested a settlement. I realized that the visit was semi-official and would safeguard me from any blackmail, but I decided to teach Yehia his lesson and also to get to the bottom of the matter.

When the case was due for trial I was again approached and advised to settle the matter out of Court. The suggested settlement had risen slightly at each stage, but the rise had not been immoderate. However, I requested that the matter should be settled in Court, as it was not my direct concern and was an affair for my groom to face. The case was fully tried and judgment was given against my groom, with a fairly heavy fine. An additional amount, corresponding to "costs", was added, and Yehia was given a full and written statement of the case and the findings of the Court.

Yehia was further told that if I personally had been concerned the fine would have been far heavier, and it was evident that it was intended I should hear that caution. My comment on the case was that it had been fairly tried and that the judgment was severe, but as everybody knew that I would pay Yehia's fine there was little doubt that the case had been conducted with scrupulous fairness and with common sense.

In my secretary's case he was advised to settle the matter out of Court. When he refused he won his case but found his award considerably smaller than if he had accepted the good offices of his friends. The deficit seemed to represent "costs" of very moderate amount.

THE QUEEN OF SHEBA

I learned that the women have their own Court, in which all cases of purely feminine interest are tried. From such inquiries as I made I learned that the system is satisfactory, but there is a general impression that the Women's Court awards more severe sentences than the Men's Court.

From the little I saw of Yemen legal administration I formed the opinion that the laws of the country are straightforward, fair, and do not interfere with the liberty of the people to anything like the same extent as the laws of Western lands.

CHAPTER XI

THE LAND OF SHEBA

To the ruler of Sabbaea, a settled country with well-established laws and prosperity, Suleiman sent his final letter by the hand of Hudhud. Hudhud means Lapwing, and the name gives the explanation to a fable that has been current for several centuries.

The Authorized Version of the Old Testament states that Suleiman spake *of* the winds, the birds, and trees. The Holy Q'ran mentions the same tradition, but more in accord with the belief prevalent in the Middle East, for the Holy Q'ran says that Suleiman spake *to* the wind, the birds and the trees, and gives the impression that Suleiman understood their languages. The explanation is that in the days of Suleiman it was customary for certain sheikhs and tribes to adopt the names of birds, winds and trees for their own tribal use.

Hudhud was probably a sheikh of one of the tribes which specialized in what we should call a postal system. These news-carrying organizations seem to have existed among the Arabs from time immemorial. Though a Turkish system of telegraph gradually displaced the

THE LAND OF SHEBA

older system, the Arabs of the present day frequently supply racing camels, dispatch-riders, and runners, who deliver messages very quickly.

There are still some legends about the marvellous swiftness of communication in the days of Suleiman. Hudhud, Ludha and Lokwan are three of the names preserved in history. Hudhud crossed from Mareb to Jerusalem in six days, Ludha and Lokhwan brought the throne of Bilkis to Palestine in the twinkling of an eye. Suleiman visited Bilkis at Sanaa and at Mareb every three months, spending the night in Sabbaea and returning to Palestine with the dawn.

"The Arabian Nights" tales of magic seem based on these legends, but when we examine legends we often find there is truth at their foundations.

Hudhud may have passed from the area of Sabbaean influence to the borders of Palestine tribes within six days. That is hard to believe, but does not present impossibilities. Ludha and Lokhwan probably did produce a replica of the throne of Bilkis in the twinkling of an eye, for that is a phrase used in Arabia as in Western lands. Suleiman may well have communicated with Bilkis between the hours of sunrise and sunset, for smoke-signals and heliograph have been employed since time immemorial. While on the duty of slave-trade prevention and also when searching for gun-runners, I have often been outwitted by smoke-signals from hill-tops.

Hudhud, the ambassador who bore the letter from Suleiman to Bilkis, must have been a capable courtier.

TREASURE OF OPHIR

The letter, though full of polite phrases, was a direct summons from the king of an upstart kingdom demanding the presence of the Queen of the Sabbaean Empire, for whilst the kingdom of Palestine had only been established some eighty-seven years and was no more than a collection of petty bedou tribes until that date, the kingdom of Sabbaea had been established at least five hundred years.

At this stage the evidence of the Holy Q'ran is very informative, and, of course, its Arab history is entirely reliable.

With the exception of Tamrin, the Merchant Prince, the advisors of Bilkis were extremely hostile to the letter. Tamrin had visited Palestine and had probably been a Sabbaean envoy of some former mission. Tamrin emphasized the wealth of Palestine and the happy condition of its people, until Bilkis pleaded with her ministers and at last gained their grudging consent to do as she pleased. She then informed them that she would first test Suleiman by sending him a further present. If he rested content to accept the present it would show he was merely a man to be tempted by wealth, and the military strength of Sabbaea was sufficient to resist the invasion of a mere plunderer. If, however, he was a prophet with all the wisdom that reputation granted to him, he would not be satisfied with presents of wealth. While agreeing to this, the ministers added that certain "hard questions" should be sent with the gifts to Suleiman.

THE LAND OF SHEBA

On his arrival, Hudhud was hospitably treated, for that was the custom of the country, but we can picture his weary wait while these negotiations were being brought to conclusion. I have seen a political mission from another Arab State being treated in a similar manner. First the members were offered full hospitality: a good house and garden were placed at their disposal, whilst their hosts busied themselves providing the best furniture and food. After three days' rest, diplomatic views were exchanged. Then matters seemed to hang fire and the visitors grew impatient, feeling that their mission was not making headway, but they frequently received invitations to visit the beauty spots of the locality, and the hospitality on such occasions shows a kindliness amazing to a European.

On one occasion His Highness the Imam invited me to a picnic at a grape-growing district. A deputy host came to ask me what I should like to take with me. Would I not like to take my European furniture? Would I care to have my own cooking utensils with me? Every possible suggestion was put forward to enhance my comfort, but since I am used to trekking at short notice, all this solicitude was rather embarrassing. However, I took with me all my outfit, expecting a two-days' trek and perhaps several days of camping. A large caravan arrived for my luggage, and we started several hours later. I was amused to find that the journey was only three hours' ride and that a house had been furnished for me to stay in as long as I liked, while the mules of the caravan were kept in readiness to return at any time I chose. I stopped the night, and after a delightful visit returned next day, to find everything had been replaced, and that my house was in perfect order.

Many such jaunts as that must have been offered to Hudhud whilst the Court puzzled out the "hard questions" which were to tax the wit of the Wisest Man in the World.

I have frequently noticed that if you ask questions the Arab can be the most secretive of men, but if you ask no questions your lack of curiosity goads him to share all his secrets with you. He blabs out his information in moments of expansiveness, and if you do not emphasize the fact that you have already heard all his secrets he will continue to retail them to you as being confidential information of the highest value. There seems no doubt that Hudhud learned the hard questions long before they were propounded to Suleiman, but it is not so certain that he knew the Sabbaean answers, if, indeed, they had been formulated.

The Sabbaean Mission consisted of one or more ambassadors, several giants, and at least ten slaves of each sex. Some historians have confused this mission with the larger one that Bilkis took to Palestine, so they have put the number of slaves as five hundred of each sex. The giants were probably of the Adite tribe, who lived in what is now known as the Aden Protectorate. Each slave took with him, or her, two golden "candle-

THE LAND OF SHEBA

sticks", which were probably the small but heavy lamps for burning mustard oil, such as are still sometimes used in the coffee-houses of Yemen. The slaves also carried bars of gold and three jewel-caskets.

Three "hard questions" were formulated for Suleiman to answer. Firstly, he would be asked to distinguish the sexes of some slave children, who would all be dressed alike.

Secondly, he would be asked to say what jewels the three caskets contained before he opened them.

The last question seemed the hardest of the three, for he was asked to give Bilkis something that came neither from the earth, nor the seas, nor from the Heavens.

The mission at length proceeded on its way, and we have evidence that Hudhud was able to give warning of the questions, for as the mission reached Palestine they met some horses and cattle tethered to golden stakes and laden with bars of gold. These golden stakes seemed so plentiful that the Sabbaean leader gave orders to his mission to throw away all their gold presents, which could be of no value in a land where even the cattle were tethered to gold pins.

That cancelled one of the hard questions, the one about the treasure, and abolished the suggestion that Suleiman could be bought with treasure. He still had two questions to answer and he made short work of them.

There are two answers given for the riddle of the

TREASURE OF OPHIR

sexes, and as this riddle was repeated by the Queen of Sheba I give only one answer here. Suleiman made the children sit down, and the spread of the knees gave him his answer, for a boy may sit with knees crossed or pressed together, though that is not a natural position for a girl to assume.

When asked to give something which came neither from Heaven, earth nor sea, Suleiman sent a horse galloping, and when it returned he ordered the perspiration to be gathered and sent to Bilkis.

Suleiman refused all offers of treasure, pointing out that his own lands offered him abundance of wealth, but he repeated his request that Bilkis should visit him, and Bilkis acceded to it, declaring publicly that she was enchanted with his letter. This brings us to the stage when the great Queen of Sheba set out with her huge caravan from the lands of Sabbaea to make the most famous journey in history.

Her fleet, with all its costly presents, set forth from Ophir, which fact is plainly shown by the specification of the fleet cargo, denoting that it was particularly composed of goods from Ophir lands, whilst the other gifts which were not carried by the fleet were from Sabbaean trading outposts. The Queen of Sheba went from Mareb to Sanaa and then down to the lowlands by a caravan route which is still in general use. There is a strong tradition that she visited Aden, and this is probably correct, for Aden would have been a good port for the final organization of her fleet and caravan.

THE LAND OF SHEBA

Having travelled backwards and forwards on this old route, I should incline to the belief that Bilkis herself did not go to Aden, but branched off at Taiz, but as tradition is so strong regarding her stay at Aden we must assume that the port was so important in those days that political demands took her there. I have failed to find any description of her journey down the old caravan route, but local conditions have remained almost unchanged through the ages and the trade winds are the same, so that we have a great deal of reliable information on which to reconstruct the details of her journey.

In all agricultural lands there is a feast-time after the harvest has been gathered. In Yemen the harvest is gathered during September, and in the highlands it commences about fourteen days earlier than in the lowlands. September would, therefore, be a convenient time for Bilkis to leave Mareb or Sanaa. The North Monsoon sets in the Indian ocean about October, and sets fair by the end of that month. So, while Bilkis was starting with her caravans from Mareb, the fleets were preparing at Ophir for their journey to Aden, which they would undertake with a following wind.

Sanaa was the capital of the Azal province and at that time was called the City of Azal. It was, as it still is, an important town, and is situated in a fertile plain ringed with mountains. These mountains give a good rainfall to the plains, and there is also plenty of sweet water both for the town and its plain. Bilkis probably stayed at Sanaa for the greater part of one

TREASURE OF OPHIR

month, which would be occupied with feasts and leave-takings to the chiefs of one of her most important provinces. Then, leaving Sanaa late in September, she set out for her journey to Aden by a route which would occupy some three weeks of leisurely travelling. It has taken me twelve days when travelling fast.

Her fleet had four or five days' cruise from Ophir to Aden direct, so they could time their arrival to coincide with the arrival of the caravans from the highlands. Western artists have portrayed the Queen of Sheba riding a camel all resplendent with gold trappings. But she probably started her journey on a white donkey and did not use a camel until she came to the lowlands, for the camel is a comfortable beast of transport on the level, but in hill country its gait is too unpleasant for leisurely travel. Further, the camel is very slow, and on the stages of the highland route Bilkis would have required a faster mount. Mules were rare in those days and were probably unknown in Sabbaea. Horses are troublesome for trekking, but the donkey is very satisfactory, and the white donkey is considered the best and strongest mount.

Some three thousand years later, using the same form of transport as Bilkis, I left the southern gate of Sanaa while the morning mists were rising and the city was stirring to its daily toil. His Highness the Imam of Yemen, with his invariable hospitality, had furnished me with a full escort and caravan. The first stopping-place was Heziaze, and shortly before we reached that

THE LAND OF SHEBA

place I had my last glimpse of Sanaa. The road had a gentle upward incline, and I turned in my saddle to say good-bye to one of the most beautiful cities in the world. It lay nestling under Jebal Nokum, a jewel of architecture with its mosques and minarets of white and red stone.

In the days of Bilkis it is said that Sanaa held thirteen hundred Himmiarrite mosques and thirteen hundred baths (Turkish baths). The number sounds excessive, but there is evidently some foundation for the legend since the baths are the same number as the temples: probably the true number has been multiplied by ten. I have examined the ruins of Himmiarrite mosques at Sanaa, one of which is sufficiently free from modern buildings for us to gain some conclusions. In Sabbaean worship the temple and bath seemed to have had direct connection, and probably all devotees washed before commencing religious rites. A city of one hundred and thirty temples was a large one, but by no means too large for the site, and for the water supply of the Azal plain.

From Heziaze I journeyed to Waalan: I did not find any Himmiarrite ruins there, but the Wazir had explained that all the ruins on the direct caravan route have been re-employed in modern buildings, although Himmiarrite remains are plentiful all along the route, a few miles distant from the main road. We reached Waalan by sunset and were very glad to settle down at the rest-house.

TREASURE OF OPHIR

In the days of Bilkis, Waalan was an important town, one of the distributing depots between Azal and the lowlands. It is difficult to realize that the little village, with its few poverty-stricken houses, represents a city of past glories. As we resumed our journey the following morning there was nothing to remind us of the feverish activities and past prosperity of Sabbaea. Where Bilkis would have travelled a road crowded with commercial life, packed caravans, and busy merchants, we passed along miles of caravan route, meeting only the humble bedou with a string of five camels loaded with maize fodder for Sanaa. Now and then we passed a boy with a donkey and pannier filled with eggs, chickens, or some such humble merchandise. The only representative of Tamrin, the merchant prince, was a modest country gentleman on a very small donkey, and he carried as a sunshade an umbrella that would have hardly been a credit to a music-hall low comedian. Rising from Sanaa, which lies 7,500 feet above the sea-level, we climbed the mountain pass of Jebel Anis at 9,500 feet, with the mountain crest towering another 500 feet above us. Jebel Anis is one of the mountains from which Bilkis brought to Suleiman precious stones, blue, mauve and red cornelians, for the priestly vestments of his Temple attendants. From the mountain-pass I looked down upon the rich plains of Belad el Jeharan and sighed for those days of past prosperity which could so easily be restored to Southern Arabia and, indeed, to the whole of the Arabian Peninsula.

THE LAND OF SHEBA

The mountain valleys of Yemen are very fertile and yield a grain supply far in excess of native requirements, but the people have allowed their roads to fall into disrepair, so that nowadays they cannot get their harvest to distributing ports at an economical figure.

My road lay southwards, taking us a two-days' ride through good grain-growing valleys and past picturesque-looking towns, such as Maaber, Dhamar and Yerim. A few years ago the journey from Sanaa to Yerim could be taken in a motor, and only occupied some six hours, but at present it can only be accomplished by a mule caravan, which takes a full three days to do the same distance. To appreciate the beauty of the land this old-time system is excellent, but for the prosperity of the country and for the betterment of the people I should like to see the motor-lorry churning the dust of these old highroads—roads now so restful . . . and so stagnant. I have lived with my Arab friends for years on end; they are hospitable to me, allowing me to share their joys, but inevitably I see their sorrows. They sigh for the prosperity of the days of Bilkis; yet they cannot put the clock back, and they are unwilling to let it go forward. When they repair their roads and make them suitable for modern requirements they will no longer be isolated from prosperity.

All along the route we met water-cisterns, disused and out of order. They are said to be Roman works, but, as I have already pointed out, the Romans can have

TREASURE OF OPHIR

done little beyond repairing systems that had been founded by earlier Governments.

We were still keeping to an average height of 9,000 feet, and at that altitude, with the bright Arabian sun, the first cooling whispers of the North Monsoon, and with the bracing mountain air, I found journeying very delightful. After Yerim we climbed the Jebel Sumara, which runs up to 10,000 feet. The road over the Sumara mountain is very precipitous, and I expressed surprise that the Turks had not cut a more gradual gradient when building a military road. My host, the innkeeper at Menzil Sumara, laughed and answered that one could not expect everything from a woman. Pressed to explain, he assured me that this road was built long before Turkish days, and local tradition held that it had been cut by a woman. It is possible that this woman was Queen Bilkis, but that is by no means certain.

At the summit of Sumara Pass we sighted the most beautiful scenery I have ever seen in all my years of travel. Hanging gardens descended like giant steps down the mountain-sides and were lost in the purple distance. On far-away mountain-slopes villages nestled like little clusters of dolls' houses. From the summit we had a steep descent of 3,000 feet to the Wadi Sukhul, and after the silence of the mountains we found the murmur of rushing torrents very refreshing. The Wadi bed is a water-course from the high mountains, and its surface is very rough; it is flanked by many

The Mosque, Ibb

The Entrance to Ibb

[Facing page 261

THE LAND OF SHEBA

trees, including the banana, which grows to a height of twenty-five feet, and giant cactus some twenty feet high. At this time of the year the tips of the cactus branches were coloured with yellow bloom. There were sycamore, fig and apricot, together with coffee-trees, which latter were in bloom and near ripening for their coming harvest.

That evening we reached Mekhader, whose waters are said to be the purest in Yemen. Here we were in a true garden land of mountain valleys, which descended gradually, following the southern stream of the Wadi Sukhul till close to Ibb. Ibb is a town built on the mountain-side, and the steep ascent is made up a path of granite steps. From Ibb at 6,700 feet we looked down upon the endless fields of a valley which lies some 5,500 feet above sea-level. The rainfall here is slight, for the bulk of the rain-bearing South Monsoon passes to the higher lands of the Jebel Sumara. Some artesian well-boring and a water conduit from the Mekhader district would give wonderful fertility to the Sukhul Valley, and, indeed, all the way from Mekhader to Ibb and Jible. Until, however, there is a motor road to the lowlands there can be no outlet for any increased fertility in this valley, which is well populated but has no large towns.

The Amil of Ibb was very hospitable to me, and the information he gave me about the prosperity of Ibb in its earlier days was most interesting. He took me to the Turkish bath, which was, of course, a great

TREASURE OF OPHIR

luxury after my long trek. He assured me that Ibb was a far larger town in the days of Bilkis, and was the capital of one of the most prosperous provinces of Sabbaea. He said that local histories told of many baths similar to the one I was using. I was surprised at the excellence of the massage, but remembered that this skill is in all probability the outcome of centuries of practice. This Arab massage work is worth keeping in mind, for it probably gives the clue to a so-called "miracle" when the presence of Suleiman cured the lameness of Bilkis.

From Jenidie, some thirty miles south of Ibb, our road turned eastward, for I was making for the Wadi Tibban. In the absence of roads it is usual to work down a wadi, which gives a fairly level route to the caravan. Previous experience had taught me the value of a good medicine-chest. I myself enjoy good health, but at every stopping-place I leave some medicine with my host, for I find that this is the most welcome of gifts. On this journey I felt somewhat like a travelling apothecary, for I was journeying to Aden and was continually booking orders for gifts, to be delivered by my guard when they returned to Sanaa.

My medical knowledge is not great, but practical experience has taught me the value of a little medicine and a lot of faith. My patients provide the faith! " He is the follower of Isa," they say, " and Isa the Prophet was the Healer of Men." For the women of the land one feels the keenest pity. The men can meet Europeans, but, as the Arab women are not allowed to

THE LAND OF SHEBA

see European men, and there are very few European women who travel to the Arakan interiors I have visited, they are unable to describe their ailments, and the explanations given by proxy are not likely to be entirely satisfactory.

On one occasion an agitated husband came to ask me for medicine for his wife. Apparently it was some slight disorder, but I suggested various aches and pains, and the husband eagerly agreed to every one of them. I prescribed some harmless remedy, with a few bread pills and many intricate instructions, which were designed to give the maximum amount of trouble and thereby increase the value of the cure. The results, according to the husband, were entirely satisfactory. Dealing with children offers unexpected difficulties to a European, for the Arab is so lax that he puts no restraint on his child. On one occasion a child was brought to me suffering from worms, a complaint which is very frequent among Arab working-classes. I gave the necessary prescription, and in order to make sure that the child should pick up no dirty food from the bazaar, I ordered that he should be kept in the house for a fortnight. The father protested that if the child was well it would be impossible to keep him indoors. I suggested that the child should be put to bed and smacked every time he got up, but the father answered that this was beyond all reason. " Very well, the child will die, so you may as well give me back the medicine," I answered, and perhaps this crude assurance may have had some effect, though I doubt if the child was kept in restraint sufficiently long to recover.

Booking my last request for medicines from our host, the Town Governor of Mawia, I crossed the frontier of the Aden Protectorate. Thereafter the road falls rapidly, for Musemir, our next stopping-place, is only some 3,000 feet above the sea-level. The rest of the journey is so well known that it is hardly worth detailed description. I accepted the Sultan of Musemir's kind offer of a car, rocketed over desert plains and into the alluvial oasis of Lahej, from whence there is a military railway to Aden. The little Arab town of Lahej is well worth a visit, for it gives a hint of the Arab interior. We passed on by car through Lahej, and through some twenty miles of dreary desert, till we reached that desolate and fly-blown Gateway of the British Eastern Empire, the barren rocks of Aden. Three thousand years ago the port was called Eden and was a place of marble baths and palm-trees. Residents would not believe in the marble baths until I found the place from whence the marble came, Shukra, some forty miles east of Aden. In my opinion the Wadi Tibban Kebir was helped by conduit across the Maala plains and led over the hills of Eden to the Tuweila Tanks, which are better known as Solomon's Tanks. In my wanderings over the desert I found some traces of this water-course, or of one more modern, which was probably a reconstruction of the ancient conduit.

At Eden, in what is now called Holkat Bay, the

THE LAND OF SHEBA

fleet of Bilkis lay at anchor. They were ships of Tharshish, and I agree with Professor Keane that Tharshish was in all probability Ceylon and has no geographical connection with Tarshish or Tarsus of the Mediterranean. It was many centuries later that the Sabbaean seamen brought their ships of Tharshish into the Mediterranean and then gave the name, a repetition which has been modified to Tarshish or Tarsus. The ships of Tharshish were sea-going dhows and very different from the light coastal vessels such as the ships of Hiram; nor were they the same as the barges that came later and were styled "ships of *Tarshish*". We gain our information by studying the cargo of the Sabbaean fleet and by cruising in the waters where that cargo was gained. Neither a ship of Tarshish nor a ship of Hiram could live in the ocean seas of those cruising grounds.

CHAPTER XII

MARRIAGE OF BILKIS

For the details of Queen Bilkis's arrival in Palestine we turn to the Holy Q'ran, the Kebra Negast, or Abyssianian Bible, several Arab histories, and the accounts in the Old Testament.

There is an amusing incident which gives a light turn to these scenes. Suleiman was anxious to learn the truth regarding this Queen, who was reputed to be a devil and to have goat's feet, so he flooded his courtyard before she arrived. She rode to the Court and was anxious to ride right up to the throne, but it was pointed out to her that the throne lay in the courtyard that was adjacent to the Temple Court, and was therefore considered holy ground. She therefore dismounted, and, finding the Court flooded, she naturally picked up her skirts to cross the water, thereby dispelling the rumour about her goat's feet.

As she crossed she tripped heavily against a floating log, and that appears to have freed the muscles of her lame foot. Probably the foot had been well massaged during her journey, and the months of travelling in the damp heat of the Tihima had brought the muscles

MARRIAGE OF BILKIS

to a sufficiently pliable state for the final stage, so that they were freed by contusion. Bilkis must have been in great pain, but she turned the incident with grace, saying that the presence of Suleiman had caused her miraculous cure. Around the log which freed the ankle muscles of Bilkis the Abyssinians have woven a complicated legend about the Tree of the Cross.

In the Middle East religion is a polite subject of conversation, in which the participants can show their learning, being mindful that religion is the source of all Eastern wisdom. It is not a tabu subject as in the West when among strangers, so that Bilkis and Suleiman easily entered into religious converse, the subject being a discussion as to whether the sun should be regarded as a Deity or only, as Suleiman alleged, an emblem of Deity. The conversation was brought to a singularly happy conclusion when, at the end of the interview, Suleiman showed Bilkis her palace, which appeared to lie across the water. Poor Bilkis looked about, but saw no boat for crossing the water, and concluded this was an indication that she was to be drowned. Suleiman showed her that the stream had been bridged with glass, and he suggested that this was an example of the danger which lay in confusing the false with the true. Bilkis replied that for the future the God of Suleiman should be her God, and we know that she was an enthusiastic convert, for in Abyssinia she gained the name of Makeda—"It is not so"—through her zeal in establishing monotheism.

TREASURE OF OPHIR

Arabs say that, in the days of Abraham, Arabia was polytheistic, but that Abraham, or Ibrahim, as he is called, destroyed the idols of Mecca. These idols were re-established, though in the days of Bilkis the people of Southern Arabia were partly sun-worshippers and partly true monotheists. The Blessed Prophet Mahomedt destroyed the idols of Mecca and re-established monotheism.

After the record of this first meeting of Bilkis and Suleiman we read a history that has a charming touch of humanity to liven its dry parchments.

For one of the "hard questions" Bilkis came into the audience-chamber bearing in her hands two bouquets of flowers. "Suleiman the Wise," she cried, "distinguish the false from the true!" Suleiman requested her to be seated, and she sat by an open window. Before long some bees came in and soon gave the answer to Suleiman.

Again we have one of Bilkis's riddles, and again we note that it has the feminine touch. From her train of one thousand girls and boys she had some dressed alike and requested Suleiman to distinguish their sexes. He sent for some basins and commanded the children to wash their hands. The little boys immediately plunged their hands into the water, but the little girls, careful of dress, first turned up their sleeves.

Considering that Suleiman had at one time a thousand wives and concubines, it is not surprising to learn that he proposed to Queen Bilkis; but it was

MARRIAGE OF BILKIS

probably something new to him to experience the rebuff of refusal. However, the wisest man on earth soon set matters aright for his own satisfaction, for he gained from Bilkis the promise that if she performed certain conditions which seemed absurdly improbable then she would consent to marry him. Though Suleiman had one thousand wives, the position was not so absurd as it would seem to Western eyes. From political necessity he needed to maintain a very large harem, and it is further suggested that he hoped to found a tribe of Royal blood. If that is so, he failed in his heart's desire, though if he had kept his promise to Bilkis he would have gained his ambition.

There was need for him to find a worthy successor so as to place his kingdom on a lasting foundation. Bilkis was a woman in a thousand, and it seems she was the one lady who really loved the great Suleiman. She insisted that if Suleiman married her she should share their Empire with equal rights and her heir should come to the throne of Suleiman. It seems certain that he accepted those conditions and then, for reasons that are not clear, was unable to keep his promise. Thereby he lost the one competent heir to his throne, and wrecked his kingdom with a broken promise.

He won his wife by an amusing strategy, for he induced her to promise that if she came to his bedside of her own accord that she would marry him. Having gained her consent, under a seemingly impossible proviso, he ordered that the evening meal was to be well

TREASURE OF OPHIR

seasoned with spices. A dinner well seasoned with fresh spices produces a thirst which is not necessarily apparent at the time of the meal but certainly develops later in the evening. Queen Bilkis awakened in the night and called for a cup of water. Her maid could find no water and went through the palace, only to return with the news that there was no water in the palace except by the bedside of Suleiman, and servants were forbidden to fetch water on pain of death. Maid and mistress then waited through the night until they felt sure that Suleiman was sound asleep.

Suleiman's sleep had a curious feature, of which they were not aware, and this was their undoing. He would lie resting with his eyes closed and at length would pass into a trance, though during that period his eyes were opened. Through the thirsty hours Bilkis and her maid lay waiting, while at intervals the maid reported that Suleiman lay awake. At length she reported that Suleiman lay still, apparently in deep slumber. Bilkis stole to his bedside and was reaching for the water carafe, when Suleiman turned to her and claimed his bride.

Bilkis kept her promise, but why could not Suleiman keep his promise? Her son by Suleiman was David, and his heirs are the ruling race in Abyssinia to this day. If Suleiman could have kept his word he would have been master of Palestine and also of the whole Sabbaean Empire.

MARRIAGE OF BILKIS

In Hebrew records it is stated that Suleiman gave to Bilkis all that she desired; yet we are inclined to ask which was the more generous of these two immortal rulers? He gave to her skilled artisans, architects, and engravers of stone, and many treasures; yet, did he truly give her all that she desired? She had given to him gold of Ophir, spices in abundance, Algum trees, Almug trees, precious stones, silver, ivory, apes and peacocks. Those were merely trading samples from her lands, and they were well balanced by the treasures of Palestine. But Bilkis gave more than these material gifts, for she gave to him his heart's desire. Yet the wisest man in the world was unable to appreciate that his ambition had been gained for him through the Queen of the South.

Finding that Suleiman would not, or could not, keep his promise, Bilkis returned, not to Arabia, but to Abyssinia. She had left Arabia against the advice of her ministers, having aimed to weld two Empires and to return to her lands as the Queen of all Arabia and of Palestine. Through a broken promise she was to return as the discarded mistress of a foreign potentate. She would not return to her capital as a discredited Queen, so she went to Abyssinia, one of her colonies. It was there she won the name of Makeda, "It is not so", apparently through her zeal in contradicting the falsehoods of polytheism. She succeeded in founding monotheism, and later on Abyssinia became the first country to accept Christianity as the national religion,

TREASURE OF OPHIR

while Makeda is revered as a saint second only to Our Lady.

In Abyssinia, Bilkis educated her son David, and when the boy came of age she sent him to Suleiman with the signet ring of his father. Reminded of his promise, Suleiman welcomed David, but once again was unable to honour the promise. David, son of Suleiman, was a man of strong character, who could have held together and expanded the kingdom of Suleiman, but instead of him Rehoboam was chosen as the successor of Suleiman. Under the disastrous reign of Rehoboam the kingdom of Suleiman was divided, and in less than a century crumbled to dust.

David returned to Abyssinia, and Abyssinian history suggests that he took with him the Holy Ark, leaving a counterfeit in its place. David of Abyssinia prospered, so that his lands have remained independent and under the same dynasty to this day. Of Bilkis, his mother, we hear little more. It seems that in the closing years of her life she returned to her old home, for her grave is at Sirwal, near to Mareb.

A Ship of Hiram

A Ship of Tharshish

CHAPTER XIII

THE CRUISE OF HIRAM

AFTER the arrival of the Queen of Sheba in Palestine, Suleiman called the vassal King Hiram into consultation. By examining the Sabbaean presents and the markets from which they came, Hiram was able to devise a trading cruise which would hold to-day, if the same goods were in similar demand.

There was the gold of Ophir, but in the present day we obtain gold from many parts of the world, and for a while the gold of Ophir is off the market. It is probable that, in the days of Suleiman, gold was won partly by driving tunnels with charcoal fires and partly by hammering lime into rock cleavages, and then wetting the lime to gain expansion. Such methods were sufficient to clean off the surface outcrops, but would not allow of deep mining. Therefore Suleiman received gold tribute from kings of Arabia and from lands where we hear of gold being present, though the natives are now unable to win it. Probably all the gold that came to Ophir was exported from there as gold of Ophir, so that it included gold from Africa as well as the Arabian gold of Havilah.

TREASURE OF OPHIR

Incense and spices are not in great demand at present, though they were extensively used in the days of Suleiman. The main incense market was from the Wadi Hadhramaut and neighbouring parts of Southern Arabia, including Shibaum, "The Land of Fragrance", near to the Dhofar district. A smaller market existed in the Island of Socotra and along the Somali coast. Incense is derived from the dwarf Dragon's Blood tree and from other gum-bearing shrubs. It is grown all along the South Arabian coast, for the gum seems to require poor sandy soil and very little rain. In the Dhofar district the best gum is called "Mghar". Please note the consonants of this name, for they give us the clue to the identity of the Almug tree, a riddle that has puzzled archæologists and Bible students for many a long year. The clue carries us further; indeed, if you will accept all our conclusions regarding "Mghar" they will in themselves give absolute location of Ophir.

Algum and Almug trees have often been classified together. In the Book of Kings it is stated that the Queen of Sheba brought Al*mug* trees, which excited admiration and were used for special purposes as "pillars for the house of the Lord, and for the King's house", and also for musical instruments. Algum trees were already known, for Hiram had sent Algum trees from Lebanon, and King David had collected Algum trees during his reign. But these Al*mug* trees excited admiration which would hardly have been awarded to a timber already known to Palestine. " There came no

THE CRUISE OF HIRAM

such Almug trees, nor were seen unto this day," is the very emphatic comment in the Book of Kings regarding the Sabbaean Al*mug* trees.

Suleiman's Temple was already built and his musicians were provided with instruments. Yet the Temple pillars were replaced and further musical instruments were made from the Sabbaean Al*mug* trees. The reason for this marked preference for the Al*mug* tree is that it was a different timber to Hiram's Algum. The Sabbaean Algum tree is a tall straight timber of hard white wood, which is practically proof against the white ant. It was particularly suitable for the white architecture of Suleiman's Temple and, being ant-proof, it was the best of timbers for permanence. Its value for musical instruments lay in the fact that it was a hard wood and therefore resonant. At present this timber is used for first-grade dhow-masts, and it was from a dhow-builder that I got full information about it. The best of this timber comes from Shibaum, slightly to north-eastward of the Dhofar district. A second-grade timber comes from the Malabar Coast, and the dhow-builder gave me this information at Makalla, while shaping the white spar he had got from the forests of Shibaum.

While the Book of Kings speaks of the Queen of Sheba's *Almug* trees, the Book of Chronicles seems to repeat the same history but refers to *Algum* trees. In a Western language the two words *Almug* and Algum sound very similar, so one is inclined to assume there has been some minor clerical error. But in Hebrew the error, if any, is a very marked one. It is the consonants which count in the Hebrew language, and those consonants could not be changed in their order, except through extraordinary error or by deliberate action. *Almug* was L-M-G, and the word is probably derived from AL M-GH-AR, denoting the greater or the distinctive Mghar tree.

In course of time the final AR was dropped and the word became L-M-G, a triliteral word of a triliteral language. But the Algum was L-G-M, an entirely different word, denoting an entirely different timber, probably a red sandal-wood (*Pterocarpus Santalinus*) or possibly a mahogany, which is also a red wood tree. It is by no means certain that there was any clerical error in the Book of Chronicles, or any confusion between the Algum and the Al*mug*. The Queen of Sheba brought Al*mug* from Shibaum and Algum from the Malabar Coasts. It was certainly the Al*mugs* which excited the greatest admiration from the people of Palestine, for they had never seen such timber, and were not likely to see it again so soon as trade with Sabbaea ceased. Hiram therefore noted Ophir as the port for procuring the *Almug* tree. Further, he noted South Arabia, Socotra and Somaliland for the incense market.

The precious stones do not give us much information, since they are not classified. Many of the precious stones of the priestly vestments are carborundums obtainable in Sabbaea. Diamonds could best be obtained

THE CRUISE OF HIRAM

from South Africa, but Sabbaea could provide a low-grade carborundum, a white rock crystal that is called the "Sanaa Diamond". Emeralds have been found in Southern Arabia, but the only Arabian emerald I have seen was of very light colour and not very attractive, though an Amsterdam jeweller had graded it as a stone of good quality.

Other precious stones in demand at that time included Agate, Amber, Amethyst, Beryl, Carbuncle, Chalcedony, Chrysolite, Jacinth, Jasper, Ligure, Onyx, Sapphire, Sardius, Sardonyx and Topaz. Some of those stones are not well defined to modern geology, but the list is so large that it gives no true assistance for location of Ophir. The Queen of Sheba brought from Sabbaea many coloured agates, and onyx was plentiful in her lands.

For the precious stones Hiram certainly noted South Africa and Southern Arabia, whilst he may have noted other markets, including the Persian Gulf, for "pearls of price", and Ceylon for moonstones. Ivory could be obtained from Africa and India. All the Somali coasts export Sudanese and Abyssinian ivories, while there is an export of ivory from all down the East African Coast. Apes could be obtained from all over the Middle East, but the best pets are the small monkeys obtained from Colombo, so it is probable that this port was his main market.

Peacocks are, of course, birds of India, and for them he would seek no other markets than India and

TREASURE OF OPHIR

Ceylon. The Hebrew word "Tuccy", with its plural "Tuccyim", has aroused tremendous discussion; but it is identical with the Tamil word which is used in Ceylon and signifies "peacock" to this day. To suit various theories the peacock has been changed into any bird short of the phœnix, though there is no reason for changing a bird of glorious plumage into some less-striking bird. The guinea-fowl has frequently been suggested. I believe the guinea-fowl is indigenous to Palestine, and certainly it is common in many districts near to Palestine. Consequently the guinea-fowl would hardly seem a bird worth importing from Ophir to a far country. Natural history is against the suggestion, especially as the peacock was easy for the Sabbaeans to obtain.

The guinea-fowl would have to be penned up for all the voyage, owing to their habit of climbing to the highest point for roosting. If they had been left loose they would have tried to fly to the mastheads and many would have been lost on the voyage. If they were penned they would take up a lot of cargo-space and there would have been many losses through sickness. There would, in fact, be no incentive to import the guinea-fowl instead of the peacock, since the peacock travels well.

By bringing into prominence one particular item of the cargo and by neglecting other equally important evidence we can develop theories to place Ophir in almost any part of the world and certainly in any part

THE CRUISE OF HIRAM

of the middle latitudes. Philology can generally give some support to any particular theory. Edouard Glaser relied greatly on the science of languages to prove that Ophir may have been up the Persian Gulf. A learned Indian professor has shown equally convincing philological evidence to support the theory of an Ophir in Ceylon. Gold of Ophir gives strong support to East African theories, or to theories of Sudan, from whence we get Abyssinian gold.

If, however, we follow out the trading cruise, we place our theory on a practical basis and pay due attention to all the evidence. We can also gain strong philological evidence to support our theories, but that evidence is not necessary to our location of Ophir. The cruising ground has been shown to include the Somali coasts, South Africa, Ceylon, and perhaps India, perhaps the Persian Gulf, and certainly the South Arabian Coast. As for the theory that Ophir was a depot from which all the goods were obtained, we must abandon such a suggestion, because it does not fall in with practical requirements.

If you were told to get ivory, apes and peacocks, gold and silver, jewels and timber of rare quality, and if you were given a seaworthy fleet and three years to complete your cruise, in what way would you start about the business? Would you go to the nearest large store and say: " Please give me several shiploads of ivory, apes and peacocks, several tons of gold and silver, some sacks of jewels, and a cargo of Almug trees?" That would

TREASURE OF OPHIR

merely be putting the work on to other shoulders, and leaving any profits for others to enjoy.

We should study the ships and the winds, so as to see the best way in which to employ them, take a cargo from our own lands, and then, by trading all the way, under the best conditions obtainable, make the most of the cruise. King Hiram had already shown himself a very practical vassal king, for he had received twenty cities in Galilee as payment for earlier work, and he had expressed himself dissatisfied with that payment. He had already organized one cruise to Ophir, which had set sail from Ezion Geber, and returned home with a cargo of the gold of Ophir. That cruise had been undertaken by ships of Hiram. They could not have brought more bulky cargo, for being small ships they had not the cargo space for heavy goods, such as Algum and *Almug* trees. Further, being small ships, not adapted for ocean cruising, they did not visit the ocean-going markets. They were, in fact, small ships which could dodge among the coral reefs of the Red Sea, since their light build and small draught ensured safe navigation in waters that were not suited to ocean-going vessels.

Once a satisfactory design has been evolved, shipping does not change. The Chinese have junks, ocean-going sailing ships, that are thousands of years old in their design. Until steamships came into general use, the British had ships of war which had reached a standard design, and had hardly altered during a hundred years. The British mercantile ship had also developed to a

THE CRUISE OF HIRAM

standard design. For the Red Sea a design, such as that of the present Red Sea fishing boat, is easy to construct, and suits all local needs. Consequently the modern Red Sea coastal boat was probably designed before the days of Hiram, and has remained unaltered to the present date.

Whilst the Red Sea fishing boat was the ship of Hiram, the ships of Tharshish were of quite a different type, since they had different work to perform, and different sea-going conditions to face. Their crews were not the servants of Hiram, and they were not the "King's ships" of Suleiman. They were, in fact, the Sabbaean Fleet. We agree with Professor Keane that their Tharshish was probably Colombo or some Indian port. The ship of Tharshish was built sufficiently heavy to stand the open sea, and was sufficiently large to be habitable for a long cruise. She was designed to sail with the wind, and to return from her outward cruise using the changed monsoon wind. Once a satisfactory design had been evolved, there was no reason why it should be changed. In an earlier chapter we have seen that shipbuilding commenced in these latitudes at some date far earlier than the Flood, consequently the ship of Tharshish had reached its standard design, and is sailing the high seas of the present day. The sea-going ships of the Indian Ocean are the ships of Tharshish, and they are best represented by the Arab dhow.

The ships of Hiram coasted down the Red Sea,

TREASURE OF OPHIR

then up the South Arabian coast, and on to Ophir. Their cruise was not necessarily a three-year voyage, though it is definitely stated that in the cruise of the Sabbaean Navy the ships of Tharshish took three years on the round trip. It is by following this Sabbaean cruise that we can trace the way to Ophir.

It has been usual to assume that the cruise for Ophir was started from Tharshish or Tarshish, which is usually located in the Mediterranean, because Paul of Tarsus came from those regions. There is little reason for assuming that Tarsus of the Mediterranean was the Tharshish of the Ophir cruise, while, on the other hand, there is strong evidence that Tharshish was east of Sabbaea. However, the exact location of Tharshish, Tarshish, or Tarsus does not concern our problem, for the Ophir cruise did not start from any such port, since its starting-point was Ezion Geber. Ezion Geber was employed on the earlier cruises, and it was employed on later cruises up to the date when the ships "were broken at Ezion Geber" in the reign of Jehoshaphat. Ezion Geber, at the head of the Red Sea, probably the great city of Zion, was situated close to the modern Red Sea port of Akaba.

There the fleet assembled about October 1st, 996 B.C. Anchored behind the outer coral reefs lay the large dhows, the "Ships of Tharshish", while further inshore lay the small coastal vessels, the "Ships of Hiram". By about October 15th, the north monsoon had set fair, and, with a following wind, the fleets set

THE CRUISE OF HIRAM

sail. The ships of Hiram took the inner passage, close to the shore, and sheltered by the coral reefs that gave safe navigation to their light draught. The ships of Tharshish kept to the deep-water track, as is used by modern steamships. Whilst the fleet of Hiram coasted

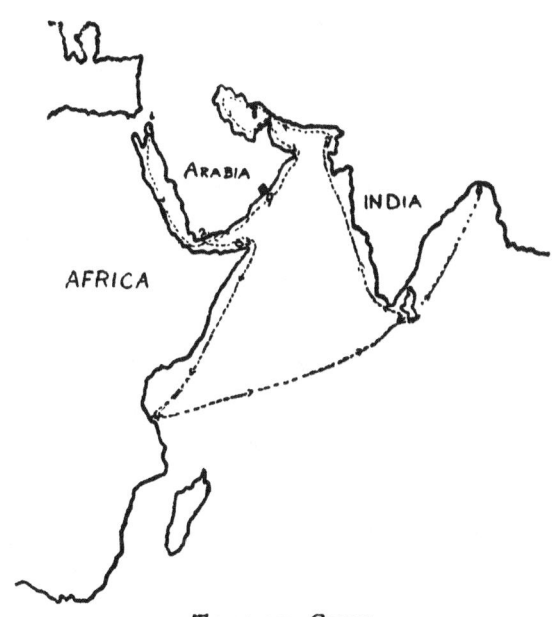

THARSHISH CRUISE

1. Ezion Geber   4. Sofala   7. Karachi
2. Aden   5. Ceylon   8. Kishm
3. Socotra   6. Calcutta   9. Ophir

down shores that are little known at the present date, they came on many a small port, as indeed I have done in those same waters.

There they could busy themselves with coastal trade

TREASURE OF OPHIR

and discharge all their cargoes. They met the ships of Tharshish at deep-water ports, such as Wej, Yembo, Jiddah, and Aden. They gave to the ships of Tharshish the fresh water and fresh provisions they had collected, and they received replenishment of their cargo from the goods which the ships of Tharshish had brought from Palestine, such as corn, wine, and the finished materials of Palestine. Palestine was by now the established manufacturing centre of the Middle East.

At Aden the two fleets parted, for the ships of Hiram continued their coastal cruise, while the ships of Tharshish took the deep-water tracks and made for the overseas markets. This Sabbaean Navy crossed the Gulf of Aden, and headed for the Somaliland coast. Somaliland, then known as the Land of Punt, yielded incense, spices, and African ivory. Socotra was the easternmost of these incense markets, and from Socotra they worked round Cape Guardafui. With the full force of the north monsoon, they cruised down the East African coast. Somewhere about Dar es Salaam they found the ancient port of Sofala, where they acquired further African ivory, and also African gold. This African gold they later brought to Ophir, but it was not the true native gold of Ophir.

They had plenty of time to reach Sofala; they needed to get there by about May, in order to refit before undertaking their return cruise with the south monsoon. About June, 996 B.C. they left Sofala with a strong south monsoon astern of them: if they had left

THE CRUISE OF HIRAM

later they would have found the south monsoon growing very strong for them. They must frequently have been sailing at a speed of ten knots, and it is curious to note that this old-world cruise from Sofala to Colombo was at a speed practically equal to the cruising speed of the modern mercantile marine. From Colombo they gained Indian ivory, apes and peacocks; also they obtained silver, Algum trees, and, perhaps, some precious stones. With plenty of southern monsoon months in front of them they had the rich coasts of India to trade with. It is true they had plenty of time, but then they also had very rich trading grounds to work in.

While part of their fleet may have worked up the east coast, and probably did so as far as Calcutta, the main fleet worked the west coasts of India, up the Malabar coast, and onward to Karachi. In Karachi latitudes the south monsoon is light, so they could work up the Persian Gulf, mainly by land and sea breezes. They evidently did so, for Kishm Island, in the Persian Gulf, has plentiful Himmiarritic remains. About November the north monsoon sets fair in the Persian Gulf, and they had till April 15th, 995 B.C., to complete half their cruising time. They rounded Ras el Hadd, the north-eastern extremity of the Arabian peninsula, and then sailed down an iron-bound coast till they came in sight of Ras Merbat. From many miles out at sea they could sight a distinctive landmark, and that is always a welcome sight to a navigator. Their land-

TREASURE OF OPHIR

mark was the peak which Theodore Bent has identified as Mount Sephar.

I visited the peak, and, without Bent's indentification, I had no difficulty in recognizing this "Sephar, a mount of the East". It is in latitude 17 5 north, and longitude 54 42 east, and this hill is now called Jebel Doan. An Admiralty publication remarks that Jebel Doan is the best landmark for making Merbat, and is a conspicuous object from the sea. On reaching Merbat, the navy was definitely in Ophir waters, for they lay in the northern harbour of the city of Ophir. Here and hereabouts they met the ships of Hiram, which they had left at Aden some fifteen months earlier.

The ships of Hiram had worked mainly by land and sea breezes. They had cruised up the incense-bearing coast, which commences at Aden and extends eastward as far as Shibaum. The ships of Hiram worked up to Bander Reisut, latitude 16 56 north, and longitude 54 1 east. This Bander Reisut is the southern harbour of the City of Ophir. According to Arab histories, both this southern harbour and the northern harbour were large seaports, flourishing apparently until long after the prosperity of Ophir had died.

Al Bilad, the city, lays half-way between Bander Reisut and Ras Merbat, in latitude 17 1 north and longitude 54 8 east. It is a city of plentiful ruins which are the ruins of Ophir, though probably they have been rebuilt many times. These ruins merely represent the

THE CRUISE OF HIRAM

citadel, palace and temple of a fair-weather city, whose population lived mainly in reed huts and light wooden buildings, which are now mingled with the dust of ages. There are many groups of ruins, which suggest the citadels of many towns that merged into this one great city, whose area was probably as great as that of any modern town.

Its sea-front was about forty miles, with southern shelter, northern harbour, and a good fresh-water inlet to the city, which fresh-water inlet gave excellent opportunity for wharfage. The city had an excellent landmark, which would give safe navigation both for day and for night. Its sea approaches were excellent and its lands are water-bearing, with water that is very sweet and good for drinking. It was open to trade with ports to north, south, and east of it; indeed, its geographical situation insured that it should become the most famous seaport in the world, at a time when its lands were inhabitated by an energetic people, who developed resources that were in demand for the world markets of the day.

Near to Ophir is the Land of Shibaum, and from the lowlands of Shibaum came incense and spices, while from the highlands came the Almug trees. From the hinterland came the gold of Havilah, which is the gold of Ophir, also the onyx stone, bdellium, and agates, which are the precious stones of Sheba.

With exactly half their cruising time spent, the two fleets of Hiram and of Sabbaea met at Ophir. They

TREASURE OF OPHIR

could return with following winds down Hazarmaveth, which we call Hadhramaut, then over to Mizraim, the Upper and Lower Egypts, onward till they reached the northern extremity of the Gulf of Suez. Always working along fresh coasts, and always sailing with a fair wind, they waited for the first breaths of the north monsoon to carry them down the desert coasts of Sinai. On October 15th, three years after they set out, they again sighted the gleaming white walls of the great city of Zion, Ezion Geber.

If you have any lingering doubts regarding Ophir, go to Al Bilad, and enter the ancient wall, either by the northern or southern gateway, and you will then find yourself in the Temple of God, where one stone still stands upon another.

A coral strand has drawn across the harbour mouth, choking prosperity from the city, but *there* ancient Ophir stands, dreaming beneath the shadow of Mount Sephar, while inland, also asleep, lies the undeveloped Transvaal of the Middle East.

THE END